BIONICLE®

Web of Shadows

by Greg Farshtey

SCHOLASTIC INC.
New York Toronto London Auckland Sydney
Mexico City New Delhi Hong Kong Buenos Aires

For Jackina, my love and my darling wife

ISBN 0-439-74558-6

12 11 10 9 8 7 6 5 4 3 2   5 6 7 8 9/0

Printed in the U.S.A.
First printing, August 2005

INTRODUCTION

Turaga Vakama carefully placed stones in the sandpit known as the Amaja Circle. The Turaga of Mata Nui had used this spot for hundreds of years to tell stories of the past or share visions of the future. But never before had any of the elders had to share so dark a tale.

He looked at the face of each Toa Nuva in turn, all of them assembled to hear his story. Then he glanced at Takanuva, the Toa of Light, who seemed as if he wished he were anywhere else. Next to him sat Hahli, the Matoran who acted as Chronicler. Vakama realized he had delayed long enough — it was time to begin.

"Gathered friends, listen again to our legend of the BIONICLE," he began, moving the stones into their proper places for the beginning of the tale. "In the time before time, six Matoran were called by the Great Spirit and transformed, made mighty Toa. These Toa Metru—myself, Nokama, Matau, Whenua, Onewa, and Nuju — risked all to vanquish our sworn enemy, Makuta."

Vakama positioned the six stones that represented the Toa so that they formed a circle in the sandpit. "We succeeded. Makuta was imprisoned, encased in impenetrable protodermis and sealed there by the combined force of the Toa's elemental powers.

"With Makuta vanquished, we journeyed to a new and wondrous home — the island of Mata Nui — a place where it seemed the Matoran could one day live in peace. All seemed well in the world. But such a victory is not won without cost. . . ."

The Turaga of Fire hurled the black Makuta stone into the center of the pit, letting its shadow fall upon the other stones. "Many Matoran were left behind, held in sway by the dark power of Makuta. We, the Toa, united in dutiful pledge, knew we would one day return to their old home, and rescue those we could not before."

Vakama glanced up at the Toa Nuva. Though he was now a Turaga, far removed from the events he was relating, Vakama let on that in his mind he was back on Metru Nui once more.

"That day came all too quickly," he said, sounding like the Toa he had been. "But the journey would not be an easy one for the Toa Metru — for Makuta did not leave the slumbering Matoran unprotected."

Gali Nuva suppressed a shudder as Vakama continued. "Their resting place was guarded by creatures of the night, hordes of the shadows, those that would poison and deceive any traveler true of heart. Their name alone was enough to strike fear: Visorak."

The Toa Nuva's eyes were drawn to the pit. The Makuta stone had pierced the rock below the sand, and now a spiderweb of cracks had formed, threatening to topple the Toa stones. Vakama smiled grimly at the sight, and resumed his tale.

Toa Onewa saw the ground rushing up toward him far too fast. Instinctively, he let his body go loose as he prepared for impact. He hit the muddy coastline of Le-Metru hard, skidding across the slick beach before finally coming to a stop.

"Well, *that* stunk," he grumbled.

A figure suddenly rose from the muck, its silhouette outlined against the pale light of the moon. Its abrupt appearance made Onewa jump. Only then did the figure scrape away a coating of seaweed and mud to reveal the mask of Nuju, Toa Metru of Ice.

"It would appear there was error in our transport," he said. "*Pilot* error."

Toa Matau's head burst from the rubble between Onewa and Nuju. He had been steering their boat, the *Lhikan II*, when it was caught in a storm and wrecked off the shore of Le-Metru. "Hey, I was order-taking," he said, annoyed. "Vakama was the one order-giving."

"No need to be so critical, Matau."

All three Toa Metru turned to see Nokama emerging from the surf. In her natural element, she was quite a striking figure. "Regardless of how gracefully, we made it here," she said softly.

"Yeah," Matau replied, still irritated. "Well . . . whatever." Then, realizing he was still pinned, he added, "Uh, could somebody dig me up?"

Before the other Toa could react, an earth-shock drill cleared away the rubble around Matau. A black-armored hand grabbed the Toa of Air and pulled him free. Matau looked up at the mask of Whenua and said, "Thanks."

The Toa of Earth shrugged. "It's what I do."

The five Toa stood together, still a bit shaken from their experience. None of them brought up the fact that Vakama was missing, fearing that perhaps he was not just absent, but dead. Their unspoken questions were answered by his voice, booming out from behind them.

"Are we going to stand around all night?" demanded the Toa of Fire. "Or are we going to rescue the Matoran?"

Matau walked slowly through Le-Metru, surrounded by his fellow Toa but feeling very much alone. Gone were the sounds of Matoran at work and play, replaced by the cries of strange Rahi. All around them were buildings damaged by the quake, places Matau had visited countless times when he was a Matoran. This city no longer felt like home but rather a place out of a nightmare.

The Toa had already caught glimpses of some of Metru Nui's newest inhabitants, vicious spiderlike creatures that seemed to be hunting down anything that moved. Now as they traveled through a city shrouded in webs and fog, Matau struggled to keep his spirits up.

"What's with all the fog?" he asked for the fourth time in as many minutes. "It's not exactly encouraging my Toa-hero spirit."

Suddenly, he stopped dead in his tracks. In the distance, the skyline of Metru Nui had become visible through the mist. The lights of the city were largely extinguished. Translucent webs glowed in the moonlight, swaying in the harsh breeze. The next moment, a herd of massive beasts stampeded across the Toa's path and vanished into the darkness.

"Whoa," said Matau. "What was that?"

"The Archives must have been breached," Whenua answered. His tone of voice was enough to say that this was a very bad thing.

"What did you have in there?" asked Onewa. He knew the answer, of course, but Po-Matoran traditionally liked to pretend that the Archives either didn't exist or were too unimportant to worry about.

"Everything," Whenua replied, too worried to be annoyed at his friend. "Most of it dangerous."

"Rahi," Vakama added, as if somehow the others might have forgotten what the Archives had been created to contain.

Whenua began to recite the opening lines of

the Archives tour he had given a hundred times as a Matoran. "The Onu-Metru Archives house a specimen of every Rahi beast ever discovered —"

His speech was cut off by a growl coming from somewhere off in the shadows.

"At least, it used to," he finished.

A gust of wind blew away the fog for a moment, revealing an Archives annex entrance. The gateway was split open and the entire structure covered in webbing. Then the fog closed in, hiding the disturbing sight once more.

"And the webs?" asked Vakama.

"Visorak. Nasty creatures," replied Whenua. He knew why Vakama was asking. The Toa Metru of Earth had only recently recalled having seen something about the Visorak in the Archives, but he had remembered too late to keep the Toa from being cornered by the creatures. They had barely escaped that trap, and Vakama was still upset that Whenua had not warned them sooner.

"Coming from you, that . . . well, it's not good," said Onewa.

"I've never heard of such creatures," said Nokama.

"Most haven't," Whenua explained, glancing at Vakama. "They're not from around here . . . originally."

"Well, there goes the old neighborhood," Matau muttered.

Nokama looked at her friends. She could not recall ever seeing them looking so uncertain in their course of action. All except Vakama, of course, who had been impatient to keep moving since they arrived back in the city. "An unexpected and unwelcome turn of events," she agreed. "But what does it change?"

"Nothing," Vakama snapped. "We go to the Coliseum. We rescue the Matoran. We leave."

"Or get pulverized," Whenua interjected.

No one spoke for a moment. Then Nuju said quietly, "It *is* a possibility."

"We've faced down Makuta and won — I really doubt a few crusty relics are going to give us much trouble," said Vakama. "Agreed?"

The others considered his words and, one by one, nodded. What choice did they have, after all? Turning back would mean dooming the Matoran to the mercies of the Visorak, and privately they all doubted the Visorak had any mercy in their hearts.

"All right," said Vakama. "Follow me."

The Toa of Fire had taken only a single step when a spinning wheel of energy flew out of the darkness and struck him square in the back. Instantly, a numbness flooded his limbs, leaving him unable to move. Five more appeared in rapid succession to strike down each of the Toa Metru in turn.

"Can't . . . move," said Vakama.

Whenua, unable to maintain his balance, began to topple forward. "Can't stop!"

"This is gonna hurt," said Matau.

The Toa of Earth fell, knocking over the others. They lay in a heap on the ground, Vakama at the bottom. "Is everyone okay?" asked the Toa of Fire.

"Paralyzed," answered Nuju. "But otherwise unharmed."

"Yeah, we're right behind you, fearless leader," Matau said mockingly. "Literally."

"Bickering won't get us out of this, Matau," Nokama said.

"No, but think-talking before charging straight into a trap might have."

"If you have something to say, Matau, say it," Vakama growled.

"Forget it," Matau replied. "I've got bigger problems."

Noises came from out of the darkness, scratching, scuttling noises that sent chills through the Toa. It sounded like a legion on the march, coming to surround the helpless heroes.

"What's that?" whispered Onewa.

"We'll soon find out," Nuju replied.

Ill-defined shapes in the mist moved closer and closer, finally emerging from the fog. Keelerak, the green-hued breed of Visorak spider, crawled into the clearing, their mandibles gnashing. Launchers mounted on their backs held spinning wheels of energy. Everything about them was revolting, as if they sent out some psychic poison that churned up every dark emotion in those who saw them.

Unable to move his head to see them clearly, Matau said, "Let me guess — Visorak?"

"Yes," answered Whenua. "In their tongue, 'the poisonous scourge.'"

"Do they even have tongues?" asked Onewa. "All I see are teeth!"

Seeing that the Toa were no longer any threat, the Keelerak began to close in. Nokama wanted to scream as their very presence filled her with an emotion beyond horror. Instead, she glanced down at the Toa of Fire. "Vakama, what do we do?"

But Vakama had no answer. All he could think of was that he had led his team into a situation they could not think or fight their way out of. His failure meant that not only they, but all the Matoran trapped beneath the Coliseum, were doomed.

"I don't know," he said quietly. "I don't know."

A lone Visorak crawled swiftly toward the Coliseum. It struggled not to surrender to a run, for that might be seen by other members of the horde as a sign of weakness. Instead, it did its best to look purposeful but not panicked.

It scuttled through the gateway and into a massive hallway lined with silver spheres. The Visorak had discovered these in the vaults below shortly after taking possession of this structure. The spider creatures were at first unsure of what they were, but Sidorak, king of the hordes, had instructed they be treated with care.

Sidorak. The name reminded the creature of just why it was in such a rush. If Sidorak learned the news from some other source, he would be sure to take it out on his unfortunate courier for being late. Or worse, he might turn the offending Visorak over to Roodaka for her amusement.

The Visorak reached the throne room. Sidorak sat in the chair once used by Makuta, master of shadows and mentor to the horde king. He looked at the approaching creature with a combination of boredom and cruelty in his eyes. "It's nothing important, I hope," he said. "Seeing as you're *late*."

The Visorak courier bowed and began to gnash its mandibles together, conveying in its native language that there was news to share.

Sidorak leaned forward. "This had better be good."

The spider creature took a breath and made a single, sharp sound. It was enough to get the horde king's undivided attention.

"Toa?" Sidorak said. "So they have returned for the Matoran — Matoran that now belong to me. I assume your telling me this without twitching uncontrollably means the Toa have already been captured?"

The Visorak nodded in the direction of the great window that dominated one wall of the room. Sidorak rose to look out over the city he now commanded. His eyes immediately focused on a new element that had been added to the scene: six cocoons, each containing a Toa Metru, hanging suspended from web lines far above the streets of Metru Nui.

"Thank you," said Sidorak. "Kill them."

The Visorak nodded again and turned, happy both to follow the order and to have an excuse to leave the throne room. Sidorak was known for his sudden changes of mood and might reward a Visorak one moment and crush it the next. The creature had almost made it to the exit when a new voice brought it up short.

"Is it to be so simple, Sidorak?"

The Visorak courier did not dare turn around. It knew to whom that voice belonged. Every member of the horde knew, and feared, Roodaka, and with good reason. But in Sidorak's eyes, she was a figure to be trusted and coveted.

"My queen," he said, reverence in his voice.

"No, not your queen," replied Roodaka. "Not yet."

"Of course. Formalities," said Sidorak. "You have something to say?"

"Only that leaders are judged by the quality of their enemies. History teaches us this."

It took Sidorak only a moment to realize to whom she was referring. "The Toa?"

"A fantastic adversary, my king," Roodaka said, gesturing to where the six hung helpessly, watched by Visorak on every rooftop. "Worthy of your rule — and therefore worthy of a demise that will be remembered for all time."

Sidorak considered. Now that he sat on the ebony throne, he found that it suited him well. True, it did not really belong to him — it was Makuta's rightful place, after all — but the master of shadows was not here, and Sidorak was. Perhaps, with the right additions to his legend, a Visorak king could hope to become much more. After all, where was it written that the shadows could *only* serve Makuta?

He smiled. "I suppose I could allow the situation to become more . . . legendary."

"I have always admired your judgment," Roodaka hissed approvingly. "Only be sure your method allows for some proof. For posterity's sake ..."

"Proof?"

Roodaka's answer came in a voice as cold as the ice that capped Ko-Metru Knowledge Towers. "Bring me their bodies."

Atop the Coliseum, Visorak jostled for position. After days of capturing nothing but Rahi, finally there was to be an "M and D" (mutation and disposal) worth watching. Toa were a rare prize — most were too smart to walk into a Visorak trap, or strong enough to fight their way out of them. Fortunately, for all their victories, these Toa Metru were evidently still new to their roles and prone to making mistakes.

One too many Boggarak tried to secure a good viewing position. When the Oohnorak next to it refused to move, it gave a shove and sent the spider creature tumbling into space.

Toa Whenua watched this happen from his unique vantage point. He would have gladly given up his place for a Visorak, if he'd had the opportunity. But it was unlikely any of the horde would want to be hanging miles above the city in a web cocoon, dangling precariously from a web line, as Whenua and his fellow Toa now were. Whenua watched the Visorak fall through a narrow gap in the webbing until the creature was lost from sight.

"That's encouraging," he muttered.

Matau glanced toward where Vakama hung, shrouded by webbing. "Well, fire-spitter, we can't say you didn't show us the city," he said, his voice rising in anger. "Course, we can say that you got us captured, poisoned, and, seeing as I don't think we've been brought up here for the view, imminently smash-dashed!"

Onewa was about to say something when he noticed the strands of webbing that held his cocoon to the line were beginning to give. When he did speak, it was muffled by the webbing that covered his mouth. "Mmmmpfff!"

"He agrees," said Matau.

"This is not Vakama's fault!" snapped Nokama from her cocoon. When four pairs of eyes all shot skeptical looks at her, she added, "Well, not entirely."

"Don't bother, Nokama," said Vakama. "I tried to lead you as best I could. I wish I was better at it, but if I've learned one thing from all we've been through . . . it's that I am what I am. And no matter how much I might want to, I can't just change."

A spasm shot through the Toa of Fire's body at that moment. An instant later, a bizarre-looking limb burst forth from his cocoon. It was a twisted mix of a powerful Toa arm and something other, something that horrified the other heroes of Metru Nui.

From the balcony of the Coliseum, Sidorak and Roodaka watched as Vakama's transformation began. Smiling, the viceroy of the horde slipped a hand onto Sidorak's shoulder, signaling her approval of the nightmare to come.

Now the strange metamorphosis was spreading to the other Toa as well. They jerked and spasmed inside their cocoons as the venom of the Visorak changed their bodies and minds. Their masks stretched and fused to their faces, their limbs grew more powerful, even as their minds were flooded with raw fury.

"I'm not liking this!" shouted Matau.

Nuju glanced downward. His transformation had the nasty side effect of shredding much of the web cocoon, and he could see the same was happening to the others. In a matter of seconds, they would be plunging to the ground and certain doom.

"You're going to like it even less in a moment, Matau," said Nuju.

Nokama glanced at Vakama. He had been the first to change, and so his cocoon was in the worst shape. "Vakama!"

The Toa of Fire locked eyes with his friend even as the last of the webbing shredded and fell away. "I'm sorry I let you all down," he said. Then he fell, to the sound of wild cheers from the Visorak.

Whenua felt himself losing his grip. The webbing could no longer support his increased weight. He tried to think of something profound to say before he dropped, but could only manage, "Uh . . . bye."

Matau watched as Whenua, Onewa, and Nuju plunged toward the ground. It was hard to believe this would be the last moment of his existence. He looked at Nokama, saying, "Nokama, I want you . . . no, I *need* you to know that I've always —"

But before he could finish his statement, he, too, fell. Nokama closed her eyes, preferring not to see herself follow the lead of her brother Toa. Then she fell, feeling the wind rushing up to greet her, and knowing the pavement was doing the same.

Vakama reflected for a moment that he must have gone insane. Here he was, dropping hundreds of feet to hard, unyielding ground, and he was bracing for impact. *As if that will make any difference at all,* he thought. *Even Toa armor cannot survive a fall from this height . . . and I am not even sure if Toa armor is what I am wearing now.*

He saw a blur of motion out of the corner

of his eye. At first, he thought it was one of the other Toa passing him on the way to the pavement. Instead, he felt an impact in his side as something snatched him in midair. The jarring knocked the wind out of him and the world went black.

High above, Nokama saw it happen. "What was —?" she began, before she, too, was grabbed and saved from a crushing death.

One by one, the other Toa followed, each saved by a mysterious rescuer. Matau was the last, and at the first sign of a motion blur, he shouted, "Easy! Don't snatch-scratch the armor!"

Vakama stirred. The ground was moving underneath him, but he was not walking across it. No, he was being carried by someone . . . or something. He couldn't make out quite who it was, or where they were heading.

"Wh — what's happened to me?" he asked.

His rescuer said nothing, just continued putting distance between them and the Coliseum. Vakama wondered if perhaps he had fallen out of the molten protodermis vat and into the furnace.

What if his new "friend" was some pawn of the Visorak, carrying him off to a fate even worse than death?

"Answer me. I am a Toa!" said Vakama.

The strange figure who carried him chuckled softly. "Not exactly," was the reply.

Matau woke up facedown in a gutter. He had been unceremoniously dumped there by his rescuer, who had disappeared. He lifted his head and looked around, noting that it was the middle of the night and he was somewhere in the ruins of Ga-Metru.

"Hello?" he called. "Nokama? Whenua? Nuju? Onewa?"

No answer came from the darkness. Matau shrugged and, with some reluctance, added, "Vakama?"

When no response came, Toa Matau reached up to clear the grit from his eyes. The first sight that greeted his newly cleared vision was his own reflection in the liquid protodermis pooled by the gutter. But the face that looked back at him was not that of a Toa. It was the face of a monstrous beast.

"No!" Matau shouted. His hands shot to his face, desperately seeking evidence that what he saw was not real. But it was. He could feel the rough contours of his features where once there had been the smooth, hard metallic surface of a Kanohi mask.

"But this isn't me," he said softly. Then anger rose in him — anger at the way he looked, anger at Makuta for destroying his city, anger at Vakama for leading them into the trap. He swiped at the puddle, stirring its surface and distorting his reflection.

As if it could get any more distorted, he thought. When the water had calmed once more, he could see other bestial shapes approach him. The rest of the Toa had arrived.

"It's all right, Matau," said Nokama.

Matau looked up at her, then at the others. They were no longer Toa, they were not even Matoran or Turaga. They were beasts . . . monsters . . . things out of a Matoran scare-story.

"All right?" he snapped. "You call *this* all right?"

"We're all alive," Nokama replied. "We'll find a way out. Together."

"That's what friends do," Whenua added, his tone more gentle than Matau had ever heard it.

Matau rose and turned to Vakama, thrusting his face right up to the Toa of Ta-Metru. "I don't hear *you* saying that, smelthead. What's the matter — too busy cooking up another master plan?"

Vakama stepped back, snarling, "I'm through making plans."

"Well, that's the first happy-good thing I've heard since I became ugly," Matau replied.

Nuju stepped between the two. "Regardless of how we look, it might be better if we use our energy to find out how and why we've become ... whatever it is we are."

Nokama nodded. "The sooner we do that, the sooner we can rescue the Matoran."

Matau turned to them, unconvinced. "How are we to *be* saving when we're the ones that *need* saving?"

No one had an answer. Then a voice laden

with age and wisdom broke the stillness, its source nearby yet unseen. "If you are wise ... if you wish to be yourselves again ..."

Six strange figures emerged from the shadows. Each had a face much like that of a Rahkshi and walked hunched over like a Rahi beast. The one in front was dark red, and he surveyed the Toa one by one.

"Then you will listen," he said.

Roodaka stood in the gloom of the sundial chamber. The great timing devices had stopped dead during the dual eclipse in Metru Nui — the moment Makuta had waited for had come and gone, the moment when he would seize his destiny. But the Toa had frustrated him, defeated him, and now he lay trapped behind a sealed layer of protodermis.

The ebony viceroy of the Visorak gazed at the stone in the palm of her hand. It was rough and black, like obsidian, carved by her from the outer surface of Makuta's prison. Even so small an effort had cost her much pain, for only a Toa could pierce the shell that surrounded the master of shadows without paying the price.

"Rest, my Makuta," she crooned to the stone. "Sleep, and know that as you do, I draw close to waking you."

She smiled, an expression that would have sent even the bravest Visorak running for refuge. "The Toa have returned, as you said they would. Even now, their broken bodies are being brought to me so I may drain them of their elemental powers. Powers I will use to shatter the wretched seal they bound you with and that keeps us apart!"

Roodaka gently, lovingly placed the Makuta stone into her breastplate. It began to pulse like a heartlight. "And then, there will be no need for these charades," she whispered. "Together, you and I will —"

She stopped abruptly. Her expression turned as hard as the stone. Coldly, she demanded, "What is it?"

A Visorak stepped out of the thick shadows, looking like it wanted more than anything to run.

But if the message it carried was not delivered, Roodaka would track the unfortunate spider creature down and then . . . It shuddered at the thought and began its report.

Roodaka listened intently. After only a few moments, she interrupted. "The Toa? Why do you speak of them as if they're still alive?"

The Visorak's mouth was dry. It glanced about, making note of where all the chamber's exits were. Then, very quietly, it answered her question.

Roodaka's reaction was immediate. Whirling, she smashed a pillar into dust. The Visorak backed away before she decided to vent her anger on it. But the viceroy of the hordes had no interest in one mere spider. No, her rage was reserved for a very specific group of individuals, whose name she spat out as if it were poison: "Rahaga!"

"Keetongu."

After he had spoken the word, Rahaga Norik waited for some reaction. But the looks on the Toa's faces indicated that none of them had ever heard the name before.

Onewa, at least, was willing to pretend he understood. "The key to Nongu," he said, matter-of-factly.

Norik shot the Toa Hordika of Stone a look, then continued. "Keetongu is a most honorable Rahi, skilled in the way of venoms — not to mention our only hope to stand against the Visorak horde. If you are to be the Toa you once were, it is Keetongu you must seek."

"But ... what are we now?" asked Nokama.

"The Visorak's Hordika venom courses within you," Norik replied grimly. "If it is not neutralized, it will take root ... and Hordika you will remain. Forever."

Nuju frowned. His mind had been sifting through theories ever since the strangers first appeared. Now he looked at Norik and said quietly, "Like you?"

"I am a Rahaga. Norik is my name." Then the bizarre-looking being gestured to his companions and introduced each of them in turn. "Gaaki. Bomonga. Kualus. Pouks. Iruini."

A moment of silence followed. It was finally broken by Matau, who said awkwardly, "So . . . how's that working out for you?"

"It has its moments," Norik replied. "This is not one of them."

Nokama shook her head. In the end, it didn't matter what these "Rahaga" were or why. All that mattered to her was what they knew. "Can you take us to this Keetongu?" she asked.

Iruini stifled a laugh. Norik turned and looked at his fellow Rahaga sternly. "Iruini!"

Nokama looked from one to the other. "I don't understand."

"What Iruini so inappropriately suggests is that this will be . . . difficult," Norik answered. "We Rahaga have come to Metru Nui in search of Keetongu ourselves, and there are those that . . . well . . . doubt his existence entirely."

Nuju's eyes narrowed. "And you?"

Norik drew himself up to his full height and said firmly, "I believe."

Nokama nodded. "Then so must we."

"Whoa there, sister," broke in Matau. "Shouldn't we think-talk about this? You know, grouplike?" He turned to Vakama, who was standing apart from the others. "What do you think, mask maker?"

The Toa Hordika of Fire stared into the flames. His tone of voice said that his thoughts were far away. "I say that we came to Metru Nui to rescue the Matoran. Not to hunt Rahi."

"And you have a way to do this?" pressed Norik. "Perhaps using your new Hordika powers? Powers you have not yet learned to use."

"I don't know."

"Don't know, or don't want to include the rest of us in your thinking?" Norik challenged.

Vakama turned from the fire to give the Rahaga a hard stare. Then he rose and walked off into the darkness, saying only, "Neither."

"Vakama!" Nokama said, shocked at his behavior.

Norik started after the troubled Toa Hordika. "I will talk to him."

"What about us?" asked Matau.

Norik smiled, but there was little humor in the expression. "Prepare yourselves. We've a legend to prove."

It took some time for Norik to calm Vakama and for the two to arrive at a compromise. Returning to the Toa Hordika, the pair suggested that the attempt to rescue the Matoran take priority over the search for Keetongu. All six Toa agreed that their own personal concerns about becoming Hordika permanently could not be as important as saving the sleeping victims of Makuta.

That they would succeed in rescuing the Matoran, no one doubted — at least, no one willing to speak up and say so. But that still left the problem of how to get them out of the city and to the island above. The *Lhikan II* was wrecked, and even if it hadn't been, it wasn't big enough to carry close to 1,000 Matoran. In the end, it was

Matau who suggested they gather the materials to build airships and fly the Matoran to safety.

A city overrun by Visorak and rampaging Rahi made this easier said than done. After a number of harrowing adventures, the Toa Metru did finally succeed in getting the items they needed and began constructing and hiding ships. Once the Matoran had been saved, there would be no need to delay making an escape from the city.

Despite their victory, the Toa Hordika were left more fragmented and disturbed than before. They were rapidly mastering the Rhotuka spinners they now carried, but had less luck mastering the Rahi sides of themselves. Too often, they had allowed anger to rule their spirits almost to the point of disaster. Vakama, in particular, had been filled with anger for days and had finally reached a point where he avoided the others completely. He spent most of his time wandering the ruins, straying farther away from the camp each day, as if straining against an invisible chain that bound him to Nokama and the rest. He surveyed the wreckage of the once proud city, reflecting on what the Toa were, what they had been, and what they had become.

So lost in thought was he that he sometimes forgot just how much Metru Nui had changed. With the Archives destroyed by the earthquake, every Rahi that had ever been housed there was now loose and roaming the city. A near fatal reminder of that came on one of his walks, when a savage Muaka cat sprang from the rubble to confront him. It snarled at Vakama, muscles tensed to spring and claws ready to rend the Toa Hordika.

Vakama reacted purely by instinct. He hunched down, blazer claws raised, and growled like a Rahi. There was no strategy behind his actions, just an animalistic show of strength. Even without his willing it, a Rhotuka spinner took shape in the launcher that was now part of his anatomy.

The Muaka took a step back. This creature looked like one of the two-legged ones that had captured the Rahi long ago, but it did not act like one. It acted like a beast, and a formidable beast at that. Deciding there had to be easier prey than this, the Muaka turned and disappeared into the darkness.

Vakama forced himself to relax. With enormous effort, he pushed down the Hordika in him and let his rational side return to dominance. "What was —?" he began.

"It meant you no harm."

The Toa Hordika of Fire turned to see Norik approaching. The Rahaga had been silently trailing Vakama since he had left the camp. In time, Vakama's Hordika senses would make it impossible for him to be followed.

"I beg to differ," Vakama replied.

Norik glanced in the direction the Muaka had gone. "It was just scared. Muaka are loners by nature, and uncomfortable being close to others." He gestured to Vakama. "There's a bit of them in you now."

It was then that the Rahaga noticed Vakama's Rhotuka spinner was still active and waiting to be launched. "Careful with that," he said quietly. "It's a most powerful tool."

Vakama had not even realized the fire spinner was there, but now he willed it to dissipate. Still, it gave him some satisfaction to know it could intimidate the Rahaga just as it had the Muaka.

"I certainly mean to find that out . . . wise one," he replied, with more than a little sarcasm in his voice. Then he turned and walked away, only to be stopped by Norik's voice.

"And what about your friends?"

Vakama spun on his heel, growling, "*Former* friends. If they think being a leader is so easy, they can try it themselves."

"True," Norik said, nodding. "But they won't succeed without you. Or you without them."

"And how do you know that?"

"I don't," Norik conceded. "But the Great Spirit does. *Unity,* duty, and destiny. If you Toa are to rescue the Matoran, you must do so *together.* This is something you can't change."

Vakama stared at the Rahaga for a long

moment, digesting his words. Then he turned again and stalked off into the shadows.

"Watch me," he snapped.

Norik watched him go. *Yes, Vakama, that I will do*, he said to himself. *You bear watching in these dark days, perhaps even more than you know.*

Nokama sat alone in the center of the Toa's makeshift camp, waiting for Norik and Vakama to return. She understood why the Toa Hordika of Fire was so upset — they had all been extremely harsh to him, although his arrogant attitude had almost invited such treatment. Still, understanding did not make her any less angry with him. After all, their quest to save the Matoran was not being made any easier by his hostility.

She heard the sound of someone approaching. "Vakama?"

But it was not the Toa Hordika, only Norik. Nokama was relieved to see him, but could not conceal her disappointment that Vakama was not with him. "Norik, it's good you're back."

"Vakama has a lot on his mind," the Rahaga said. "We must give him time to find his destiny."

"And if he finds a particularly bad one?" asked Onewa.

"Now then — we should begin our search for Keetongu at once," Norik replied, ignoring the question. Nokama and Onewa exchanged glances, wondering why the Rahaga did not want to address the issue of Vakama.

Matau, on the other hand, was more than happy to focus on the new topic. "Right! Keetongu! Getting turned back into our old, ever-handsome selves. Let's get on that."

"But where to start?" asked Nuju. He was still skeptical that a creature like this Keetongu could have been in the city without anyone being aware of it.

"Somewhere you know well," Norik replied. Then he walked off, followed by the rest of the Rahaga. The Toa looked at each other, then decided that Norik's abrupt departure was meant as a signal that they should join him. They rose and trailed after the Rahaga, wondering just where he was leading.

*   *   *

Some distance away, Vakama continued to walk aimlessly. He kept replaying his conversation with Norik over in his head. *Unity . . . what does that mean? Were the other Toa showing any unity when they kept criticizing the job I was doing? Okay, so I made some mistakes . . . like Onewa never has, or Matau — he's the king of mistakes.*

I did what Lhikan would have wanted me to do, he said to himself. *I put saving the Matoran first, above personal safety or anything else. It just . . . didn't work out. And considering what I learned — that Lhikan's choice of the six of us as Toa was inspired by Makuta, not the Great Spirit — why should anyone be surprised that we — I — fouled up?*

"I can do it alone," he said aloud. He pictured the shocked looks on the faces of the others when they saw that he had rescued the Matoran all by himself. "I'll show them all!"

Vakama scrambled over a pile of rubble and found himself at the edge of a steep precipice. The chutes that had once run from this spot had long since been destroyed. Now there was nothing but a view of the vast, web-shrouded city of Metru Nui. The Toa Hordika looked out over his home and was struck again by how big it really was. He frowned. What had he been thinking? How could he believe he could challenge an entire city full of Visorak alone? How would trying that benefit the Matoran?

"Who am I kidding?" he muttered. "Maybe Norik's right. Maybe I can't do this without the others. Maybe I don't *want* to do this without the others."

His thoughts were interrupted by a Rhotuka spinner whizzing past his head. Vakama leapt, rolled, and came up on his feet to find himself confronting a Boggarak, the blue Visorak that commonly stalked Ga-Metru. Vakama remembered Gaaki saying that on land, Boggarak spinners had the power to totally dehydrate a target and reduce it to dust.

"Thanks for the warning shot," he said, readying himself to dodge again.

The Boggarak launched a second spinner. Vakama evaded it with ease. The Toa Hordika energized one of his fire spinners, saying, "All right, so you've just got bad aim. Watch and learn."

Vakama launched the spinner. Just as it was about to strike the Boggarak, another spinner struck the wheel of energy and deflected it from its course. The Toa Hordika turned to see three more Boggarak closing in. With the cliff at his back, and the four Visorak in front of him, he was effectively trapped. His Hordika side rose to the fore — all Rahi hate to be cornered — and he gave a fearsome growl.

The Visorak ignored him. They were used to Rahi making threatening noises when the trap was sprung. That was part of the fun of the hunt. Their only regret was that this hunt would be over so soon, but there were still five more Toa Hordika to track down once Vakama was finished.

Those five Toa Metru stood with the six Rahaga before the Great Temple in Ga-Metru. Despite all the damage done to the city, the temple still stood proudly, as if it were a symbol of the fact that, though the Great Spirit Mata Nui now slumbered, he had not been destroyed.

"Here?" Matau asked in disbelief. "I'm sure it could have great-helped our old Toa selves, but now?"

"We'll never find a way to change back if you keep talking like that," Onewa snapped.

"You're right. I'm sorry. I don't know what's gotten into me," Matau answered, sharply. "Oh, that's right — some kind of Rahi monster!"

Norik shot looks at both Toa. "If you're quite done, we should go inside."

All five Toa Hordika hesitated. Nokama had already been back to the Great Temple since their transformation, and she remembered how hard it had been for her to enter the structure as a tainted Toa. Now the others were feeling that as well. It just did not seem right to enter — yet, if Norik was correct, their only hope of ever being Toa Metru again lay inside. Still, none of them could take that first step.

Is this it, then? Whenua wondered. *Are we already so far gone that the temple of the Great*

Spirit rejects us? And if that's true, have we already lost our fight?

Toa Hordika Vakama expected to wake up in a cocoon, or a cage — that's assuming he was going to wake up at all. When the Boggarak paralyzed him, he had fallen and hit the ground just hard enough to stun himself. Now, as he looked around, he wondered if he was still unconscious and dreaming.

He was alone in a chamber he had never seen before. His wrists were bound with thick Visorak webbing that also served to anchor him to the floor. He pulled at his bonds, but they would not give, even to his Hordika-enhanced strength.

His thoughts raced. *Confined. Trapped. Again. I hate being trapped! I hate being helpless! I am a Toa ... a Toa of Fire ... I am ... I am ... a Hordika!*

A howl split the night, a primal sound of rage and despair. For a moment, Vakama wondered what sort of Rahi would make such a sound. Then he realized with a start that it was coming from his own mouth.

"What's happening to me?"

A tall figure stepped into the room. She moved as gracefully and noiselessly as if she were made of darkness. Her face and body were as black as shadow, but her eyes blazed like the Ta-Metru fire pits. Vakama had never seen her before, but from Norik's description, he knew who she had to be.

"You are ... becoming," purred Roodaka.

"Yes, but what?"

The viceroy of the Visorak stopped in front of her prisoner. "A friend ... or a foe. That's for you to decide. It's why I have invited you here."

Vakama tugged at his bonds again. "Some invitation."

Roodaka smiled. "Then perhaps this one will be more to your liking—walk with me. I've a ... proposal for you."

Vakama's Rahi senses were on full alert, screaming that there was danger near. He chose to ignore them. "And if I don't want to hear it?" he asked.

Roodaka reached out to trace the outline of his misshapen features. "Be reasonable, Vakama."

With that, she turned and began to walk away. Then, as if suddenly remembering his condition, she waved her hand. The webbing binding him fell away and crumbled to dust.

"What harm could come from listening?" she asked, her voice as soft and cold as the winter wind.

Roodaka and Vakama stood on the Coliseum balcony overlooking the ruins of Ta-Metru. He was still not sure why he had followed her out here. Perhaps it was curiosity . . . a desire to know his enemy better . . . or perhaps it was just a certainty that she would not have freed him if there were any chance for him to escape. Or perhaps he was genuinely interested in what she had to say?

No, no, he assured himself. *That can't be it.*

The viceroy glanced around to make sure they were alone. Her voice dropped to a conspiratorial whisper. "Secrecy is such a burden, but Sidorak mustn't know we spoke."

"Sidorak?"

"King of the Visorak." She made no attempt to disguise the contempt in her voice.

"And he doesn't know you've captured me?" Vakama was unsure whether he believed all this. Norik had told him of Roodaka's talent for treachery. But why would she pretend to dislike her king?

"Not yet," she answered flatly.

Vakama shrugged. "Some leader."

"I agree."

Vakama's eyes widened. It was one thing to show a lack of respect for a king, quite another to be so open about one's disloyalty. What was this creature up to? Despite himself, he was intrigued by the sheer darkness and danger of this Roodaka.

He looked to either side. Boggarak lurked in the shadows. "You're not worried they're going to tell him you said that?"

"They are loyal to me," Roodaka replied.

Vakama almost laughed. "Right. Like you are to Sidorak?"

"Yes," the viceroy said, her tone hard. "They obey me because I am strong. They fear me, and therefore do not dare to question my authority. That is leadership, Vakama. That is how the other Toa should treat you."

She moved in a little closer, her words wrapping around him like a tentacle. "Maybe then they wouldn't say such awful things...."

He glared at her. She could read the unspoken question in his eyes. *How could she know of such things? And how much more does she know?*

"The Visorak horde is legion, Vakama, and has twice as many ears," she answered. Nearby, the Boggarak made a sound that passed for laughter among their kind.

"I trust my fellow Toa —" Vakama began.

Roodaka cut him off. "To do what? Hold you back? They're not worthy of a leader like you... which is why I've brought you here."

Vakama gazed out at the Metru Nui night. He could make out the familiar skyline of furnaces and forges, those that had survived the quake mostly intact. "Ta-Metru," he said sadly. "When I was a Matoran, it was my whole world.

It meant everything to me." He turned to look again at Roodaka. "It still does."

"It can be your home again, Vakama — to rule as you see fit. All you need to do is lead those who will obey you properly."

Leaning in close to him, she hissed, "Lead the Visorak horde!"

Norik was halfway through the entrance to the Great Temple when he realized the Toa Hordika were not behind him. He turned and saw them still standing uncomfortably a few feet from the gateway.

"Is something wrong?" he asked.

Nokama looked at the others. Having experienced what they were feeling, she decided it was best that she speak for them all. "It might be best if we wait here. The Great Temple is sacred to Toa. Given what's happened . . . I'm not sure it would be right."

Norik pondered her words for a moment, then nodded. "I understand. Our work here will not go unnoticed. I must ask that you buy us the time it takes to complete it at all costs."

"Consider it done," answered Nokama.

She turned and headed back to the bridge that connected the Great Temple to Metru Nui, the others following. Only Matau remained behind.

"Wait!" he called after them. "Don't you think we should think-talk about —"

"No!" the four Toa shouted in unison.

Outvoted, Matau shrugged and loped after his friends. He did not want to remain at the temple alone.

Better to be with my pack . . . my team, he corrected himself. *This place is full of hidden dangers now. They might come from almost any direction . . . even the one you would least suspect.*

"I . . . don't know."

Part of Vakama could not believe he was even considering Roodaka's offer. He was a Toa! He had been entrusted with power by Lhikan himself! How could he give as much as a moment's thought to the idea of taking command of the Visorak horde?

But another, stronger voice spoke in his mind as well. *I am not a Toa — not anymore — and I was a failure when I carried that burden. Think about it: Do I really think six Toa Hordika and six freakish Rahaga can overcome hundreds of Visorak and free the Matoran? How many will die in that attempt? How many Matoran will never see the sunlight on the island above?*

Vakama tried to drive away these thoughts, but they just came faster. *If I accept her offer — if I take the power that is being given me — I could order the Matoran to be freed! I could convince Roodaka to let the Toa Hordika leave with them and head to safety. And if it means I have to remain behind in Metru Nui . . . well, no one will miss me. Of that, I am sure.*

Roodaka interrupted his musings. "I understand your reluctance. You require proof."

She turned to her personal Boggarak guard and gestured toward the low balcony rail and the darkness beyond. "Throw yourself off the edge," she ordered.

Without a sound or a moment's hesitation, the Visorak marched obediently forward. To Vakama's horror, they plunged off the edge of the balcony, one by one. He rushed forward to look.

The Toa Hordika of Fire peered over the rail, expecting to see nothing but all-consuming blackness. Instead, to his surprise, he spotted the Boggarak sprawled on a ledge about ten feet below, unharmed.

"I didn't know there was a ledge," he said, relieved.

Roodaka smiled. "Neither did they."

She took a step closer to him, saying, "Obedience. This is but the first of many lessons I can teach you."

"And this is something your 'king' would allow?"

"There is a way."

Vakama made his decision then. It wasn't one the other Toa or those old fools, the Rahaga, would ever be able to understand. He knew that. But it would ensure their safety in the end, he hoped, and free him from the shadow of Toa

Lhikan. He would no longer try to be something he was not cut out for — instead, he would be a leader of a different kind.

"I'm listening," he said quietly.

Roodaka allowed an undertone of triumph to enter her voice. "Six ways, Vakama . . . six ways."

Rahaga Gaaki worked feverishly. The inscription she was translating was old and in a Matoran dialect she had not mastered. She wished she had access to Toa Nokama's Mask of Translation, but such power had been denied her for far too many years. She had to rely on her own experience and wits.

A soft sound distracted her from her work. She turned to investigate, only to see Norik entering the Great Temple chamber. "Are you all right, Gaaki?" he asked.

"Norik, I . . . I heard something."

"Probably just my approach," he said. "Age makes us loud as well as wise."

Gaaki wanted to be comforted by his words, but somehow she could not be. She knew the sound she had heard did not belong in this place. "No. This was a creature."

"Visorak?"

She shook her head, but said nothing.

"Gaaki, what did you hear?" he asked, now recognizing the depth of her unease.

"That's the thing — I can recognize everything that walks, crawls or flies in this world by sight, sound, or smell," she said, frustrated. "But not this."

Norik was worried. Gaaki was a skilled tracker, on land as well as in the water. She and the other Rahaga knew the Rahi kingdom like no one else ever had — they had to in order to survive. For her to admit being baffled, this mystery creature would have to be . . .

No. By Mata Nui, it cannot be, he thought.

Doing his best to hide his fears, he reached out a comforting hand to Gaaki. "I'm sure it's nothing. A 'glitch' brought on by processing such an elaborate translation."

"I guess I have been working kind of hard," she conceded.

"Gather your brothers and go outside. Check on the Toa," he said.

"What about you?"

"I'll be right behind you," Norik lied. "Find the Toa."

Gaaki turned and ascended a set of spiral steps that led to the temple exit. Norik waited until he could see and hear no sign of her before shifting his attention back to what appeared to be an empty room. But appearances could be deceiving, Norik knew. Creatures who seemed like horrible monsters could have good and noble hearts, and those who claimed to be heroes could be the worst villains of all. Beneath every being's thin shell of civilization, there lurked always a Rahi beast, longing to emerge. All it needed was the slightest crack to slip through into the daylight, and becoming a Hordika was more than a crack — it was a chasm.

"Show yourself!" he demanded.

Behind the Rahaga, a figure flitted from one shadow to the next. Had Norik seen it, he would have been hard pressed to identify it, for it seemed more Rahi than anything else.

"I doubt you'd recognize me," said the dark figure.

Norik wheeled. That was Vakama's voice! But the Toa Hordika was nowhere to be seen. Silently, the Rahaga thanked the Great Spirit he had thought to get Gaaki out of harm's way.

Vakama's voice came again, this time from a different corner of the room. "I've got some bad news. Gaaki's not going to find her brother Rahaga upstairs."

"What have you done with them?" snapped Norik. For a moment, he wondered if Vakama could have gone so far as to kill the other Rahaga. If he had . . . no matter the difference in their power, Norik vowed to make him pay in kind.

The Toa Hordika's reply came from yet another corner of the room. "Nothing," he said. "Yet."

Norik turned left and right, trying to spot the Toa, but his quarry had learned to use the shadows too well. "Then it's not too late, Vakama. You don't have to do this...."

There was a long pause. Then a voice that sounded more like that of the hero of Metru Nui said, "Give me one reason I shouldn't."

"The other Toa. They need you to lead them." As soon as he spoke the words, Norik knew he had made a mistake.

"It's always about what's best for the others!" Vakama growled. "She was right about them, Norik. About me."

"Who have you been talking to, Vakama? Who put these thoughts into your head?" Norik asked, though he was already certain of the answer.

"You'll find out," Vakama chuckled. "I'm counting on it."

"I don't understand."

"You don't have to understand the message, Norik," Vakama said, his tone dark with rage. "Just carry it."

"This message — what is it?"

The Toa Hordika's answer was a growl that sounded as if it had been torn from deep inside him. Norik looked up barely in time to see Vakama, now completely in thrall to his Hordika side, plunging down from above.

Then Norik saw nothing but darkness.

6

Dawn was breaking. Nokama felt the pale sunlight warming her armor and awoke. For a few seconds, she wondered what had happened to her city. Where were all the Matoran? Why were the chutes not running?

Then a flood of memory returned. Dume who was not Dume, but Makuta in disguise; a thousand Matoran forced into spheres and rendered comatose; darkness falling over the suns, the ground shaking . . .

She shook her head to clear the visions away. There were more immediate problems to worry about, she reminded herself. *If we cannot reverse what has happened to us, all that has gone before will seem like just a spirited game of akilini.*

Nokama rose and walked to the Great Temple gateway. Beyond that impressive arch was the bridge that led to the most venerated structure in all Metru Nui. Amazingly, it still stood, exactly as she remembered it. Only one thing was missing. . . .

"Matau?"

The Toa Hordika of Air had agreed to take the final shift on guard. But he was nowhere to be found. *Has something happened?* she wondered. *Could the Visorak have taken him by surprise, capturing him before he could give a cry of warning?*

Small bits of rock and wood suddenly rained down upon her. Puzzled, she looked up to see Matau in the eaves of the arch, building what looked suspiciously like a nest. After a few moments, he noticed Nokama down below.

"Uh . . . yes?"

"I thought you were keeping watch," said Nokama.

"I was."

She gave him a skeptical look, inviting him to try again.

"And building this," he continued. "But much more with the guard-watching. It was quite a night, me and the . . . watching."

Nokama gestured toward the bizarre structure of wood, mud, and stone Matau had been building. "Surely, this must be the most impressive thing ever built by an insane Toa in all of Metru Nui," she said flatly. "Seriously — what *are* you doing?"

Matau jumped down from his perch on the arch to land beside her. "That's the thing," he confessed. "I have no idea. I just had this . . . *urge*. To nest-make!"

To his surprise, Nokama did not snap at him. Instead, she looked away, saying, "I get them, too. Ever since —" She gestured at herself, then at him, and he knew she was referring to their transformation.

"It's nearly morning," she said. "We should find the others and see what the Rahaga have learned."

She headed for their makeshift camp, Matau following quickly after. "These urges," he said hopefully. "They wouldn't involve me, would they . . . ?"

*   *   *

Nokama and Matau woke up the others, and together they started across the bridge toward the Great Temple. "Norik seemed so concerned," she said. "But no one saw anything all night?"

"Nothing," Whenua said. "Lots of nothing."

"Yeah, boring," Onewa agreed.

"I don't know," Nuju said, a little bit wistfully. "I found the sounds of the night fascinating."

Matau gave the Toa Hordika of Ice a look. "Riiighhht. Anyway, I wonder what's taking the Rahaga so long. I mean, how hard is it to get directions?"

"When they're written for a creature that has not been since the time before time?" Nuju answered. "Hard."

"Be patient, Matau," said Nokama.

"I have no patience for ever-looking like this!" Matau quickened his pace, swiftly outdistancing the others. "We've already spent-wasted a whole night! The way I see it, the faster we get to —"

He stopped abruptly, too shocked by what

he saw to say any more. Then, weakly, he finished, "the Great Temple."

Now the other Toa Hordika could see it, too. The Great Temple looked like a Tahtorak had rampaged through it. Smoke wafted from the building and curled into the night sky. And all of them felt a fear worse than any they had ever known before clutch at their hearts. As one, they raced across the bridge.

The interior of the Great Temple looked even worse than its exterior. The structure had been gutted, and as they entered, much of it was still smoldering. A fine layer of ash lay over everything.

"Norik?" Nokama called. They had not seen a trace of any of the Rahaga. None of the Toa cared to voice their collective fear that their new allies might not have survived the fire.

"I can't see anything," said Nuju.

"What should we do?" Onewa asked.

Nokama looked at Matau, but the Toa

Hordika of Air just shook his head. He had no answers.

"I wish Vakama was here," she said softly.

"He was."

Nokama turned, startled. The voice was weak, but it was definitely Norik's. The Toa Hordika found him buried under a pile of rubble. Whenua immediately began digging him out. Nuju noted as he did so that the pieces of stone covering the Rahaga were fragments of the tablet Gaaki had been translating. Their best, perhaps only, hope of finding Keetongu had been shattered.

Norik looked up at his rescuers, but there was no relief in his eyes, only an incredible sadness. "He was," the Rahaga repeated.

Vakama stood at the gate to the Coliseum, banging on the massive door. By his side was a large, unwieldy object covered in a veil of Visorak webbing. He had been pounding away for some time now, unmolested by the spider creatures who seemed more puzzled than anything else by his sudden appearance.

The voice of Sidorak suddenly boomed from the Coliseum speakers. "You must be confused, Toa. We do not welcome your kind here — we exterminate it."

"It's you who is confused, Sidorak," Vakama replied boldly. "I am no simple Toa."

A gleaming telescope extended from the gate and then paused, as if studying Vakama. Sidorak knew, of course, what it would reveal, but even he was amazed at how swiftly and dramatically Vakama had changed.

"Hordika," breathed the king of the Visorak. "Why have you come here?"

"To join you."

Sidorak laughed, a sound made more terrible by the echoing of the speakers. Undeterred, Vakama shouted over it. "And to present you with proof of my worth."

The Toa Hordika of Fire yanked the webbing off his burden. Beneath the veil were the five Rahaga, bound, helpless, and about to be delivered to their mortal enemy.

Sidorak's laughter stopped. A moment later,

the great doorway of the Coliseum swung open. Vakama stepped inside, dragging the Rahaga behind him, and was swallowed by the shadows within.

It always amazed Norik how little time it took to relate events, yet how devastating the tale could be. As he looked around at the Toa Hordika, he could see how deeply shocked they were by his news of Vakama's attack upon him.

"Vakama would never do such a thing!" Nokama insisted. She turned to the others for support. "Right?"

None of the other Toa responded. It was left to Norik to extend a sympathetic hand to Nokama and say gently, "You are right, Nokama. The Vakama you know would not."

"But?"

"He's changed," said Norik. "Just as you all will if we do not find Keetongu. I fear Vakama has given himself completely to the beast that lurks within us all."

Onewa glanced down at his new body and

made a lame attempt to lighten the mood. "Beast? I'm pretty sure it's just me in here."

No one laughed.

"The ancient. The primal," Norik continued. "The parts of ourselves that we like to think progress has made us forget. 'Hordika' is its name."

"I don't think I want to be Hordika," decided Whenua.

Norik shrugged. "It's not all bad, Whenua — not if you don't allow it to be. Being Hordika grants you certain gifts, abilities you would have never thought possible before."

Nokama found herself remembering Matau's nesting, and her newfound connection to nature. Were these the "gifts" Norik spoke of? If so, she would gladly return them for the chance to be a Toa Metru once more.

"Assuming you're right," she said, "we must find Keetongu and rescue the Matoran before the beast overcomes us, too."

"Yes," Norik replied, looking away from her. "But I must warn you . . . Vakama may already be beyond anything even Keetongu could do."

"Well, we have to try," broke in Matau. "We owe the fire-spitter that much. I was kind of hard on him...."

The other Toa nodded. They had all been hard on him, even before they returned to Metru Nui. Rather than consider what he might have been going through, all they had worried about was how his behavior affected them.

"And if you cannot help him?" asked Norik.

Matau's tone grew dark. "You leave that to me."

A beat of uncomfortable silence followed. Then Nuju broke the tension, saying, "So. Back to searching."

"Not exactly," the Rahaga replied.

"Quick-speak," urged Matau.

"We were able to translate much of the inscription before Vakama's attack. It read, 'Follow falling tears to Ko-Metru, until they reach the sky.'"

The Toa glanced up at the Great Temple.

A steady stream of liquid protodermis was rolling off its carved face, like makeshift teardrops.

"It is there we will find Keetongu," finished Norik.

"Protodermis that runs upward?" asked Matau, skeptical.

"Hey, it's not much of a plan," answered Onewa. "But it is a plan."

Iruini struggled against his bonds. The Rahaga were packed together tightly and had been webbed to the facing of the Coliseum's observation deck, like trophies on display. The Rahaga looked up to see the Toa Hordika of Fire looking down upon him.

"Vakama …"

"That name means nothing to me," Vakama answered.

"It did once," Iruini said. "It can again."

"That's true. It can."

The voice was Roodaka's, coming to join her new ally. "If you want to be weak again," she added.

"Never," replied Vakama.

Roodaka looked down at her Rahaga captives without a trace of pity in her face. "Save your strength. Bait is most alluring when it squirms."

The viceroy of the Visorak smiled and placed a hand on Vakama's shoulder. "You're everything I hoped you'd be," she hissed. "Come. It's time you got a glimpse of your future."

She turned away and headed for the inner chamber. After a brief glance back at the Rahaga, Vakama followed. Iruini watched him go, wondering if he had just been witness to the final death of all hope for the Matoran.

In times past, the Toa's journey from Ga-Metru to Ko-Metru would have been a quick and simple trip through the transport chutes. Any one of a dozen chutes connected the two metru, most running near the Coliseum. But with so many chutes destroyed and the Coliseum now in the hands of the Visorak, Nokama and the others had to take a longer, slower overland route to Nuju's metru.

Upon reaching the border of Le-Metru and Ko-Metru, they found that the canal once bridged by chutes now played host to a very different kind of span. Visorak had constructed a bridge of webbing to connect the two metru. Nokama, Nuju, Whenua, and Norik crossed over immediately, leaving Onewa and Matau behind to guard the rear.

The Toa Hordika of Stone now stopped to listen. They had done their best to avoid attracting the attention of Visorak along the journey, but he was fairly certain a squad of Oohnorak had spotted them as they neared the border. The strange sounds he heard only confirmed his fear.

"What was that?" he asked Matau.

The sounds grew nearer, the scuttling noise produced by a dozen Visorak closing in on their position.

"I'll give you one guess, as long as it's Visorak," Matau answered. "Beat-feet!"

Onewa started to take a step onto the bridge, then hesitated. "You think it'll hold?"

"I don't know. But I'd rather take my chances with it than them."

"Good point," said Onewa.

On the other side of the span, Nokama turned back to see her two fellow Toa Hordika still lagging. "Matau, Onewa — hurry!" she shouted.

The Toa Hordika of Stone gingerly put his foot on the bridge. Instantly, he knew it had been a mistake. Strained beyond its breaking point, the webbing snapped violently. Onewa fell backward as Nokama, Nuju, Whenua, and Norik were launched into the air as if from a slingshot.

The three Toa Hordika managed to catch hold of ledges on the chasm wall and scramble up the other side. Nuju looked around and noticed that one member of their party was absent. "Where's Norik?"

"Up here!" The voice came from above. They looked up to see that the Rahaga was ensnared in a part of the bridge's webbing. "This is not entirely pleasant."

"Yeah," said Whenua. "Been there, done that."

Nokama glanced back over the bridge. Onewa and Matau were now effectively stranded. Worse, she could see the vague forms of Oohnorak approaching them through the mist. In a matter of moments, her two friends would either be captured by the Visorak or forced off the edge and sent plunging into the canal to their doom.

And the terrible thing is, I am not sure which fate would be worse, she said to herself.

* * *

Vakama stood in what had once been Turaga Dume's inner chamber in the Coliseum, later converted by Makuta for his own dark purposes. The centerpiece of the room was a dark, twisted throne. Even empty, there was no mistaking the fact that this was a seat of power.

"Go ahead," Roodaka beckoned. "Touch it."

Vakama reached out and let his fingers brush the throne. In that instant, his mind was flooded with shadows, images of evil deeds past and those to come, and a vast, all-consuming contempt for any who stood in opposition to his desires.

No, not my desires — Makuta's, he realized. *But in this moment, they are the same . . . we are the same. The eclipse, the earthquake — Makuta caused them by sending the Great Spirit Mata Nui into unending slumber. The Matoran and the Rahi and everything else that lives would be sealed away until such time as they could be awakened to live under our . . . under his rule. That is why the Visorak are here, that is why they have marched through and conquered land after land, and there is nothing on Metru Nui that can stop us ... them ... us.*

The Toa Hordika of Fire yanked his hand away from the throne as if the chair had bitten him. It felt as if he had been touching it and awash in its corruption for an age, when in reality only a split second had passed.

"What did you see?" asked Roodaka.

Before Vakama could answer, Sidorak entered the chamber. "You can look, Vakama, but don't touch."

Vakama turned to see the king of the Visorak approaching, flanked by two Oohnorak. Sidorak sat down heavily on the throne.

"I wanted to thank you personally," he said to Vakama. "Because of you, the Rahaga will meet a fitting end. Just as soon as I think of one."

"It is just the beginning of what he can offer you," Roodaka said softly.

"Is that so?"

"It is, my king," the viceroy purred. "Vakama is my gift to you. A fitting master for your horde."

Sidorak shook his head. As much as he

respected Roodaka's wisdom, she was wrong in this case. The horde was far too large for any one field commander to manage. "Hordika or not, there's only one of him —"

But Roodaka was prepared for this objection. "Which is why the other Toa are on their way here. With Vakama leading your horde, they will be captured and ... trained ... just like him. Will all six be enough to please you?"

"A fine offer, Roodaka," Sidorak said.

"Consider it an engagement gift," Roodaka pronounced, smiling.

"Well, then," Sidorak replied, glancing at Vakama. "We should introduce you to the horde."

Matau looped another strand of webbing around two rock outcroppings. Satisfied with what he had created, he looked at Onewa. "Come on."

"You're not thinking what I think you're thinking," said the Toa Hordika of Stone.

Matau pulled the webbing taut and tested its strength. Then he stepped into the center of the makeshift slingshot and backed up against the resistance of the webbing, stretching it out.

"Yes. You are," said Onewa, stepping over to join the Toa Hordika of Air in the center. "I knew there was a reason I always liked you."

Working together, they forced the webbing back, back, until it was strained to the limit. "Tight-hold!" said Matau.

Onewa grabbed on to his fellow Toa. Then they both lifted their feet from the ground and the slingshot snapped forward, launching them out over the chasm just as the Oohnorak burst into view behind them. Spotting Norik entangled below, Onewa reached down and grabbed him. "Going our way?"

"We did it!" shouted Matau. "We're going to make it!"

But the Toa Hordika of Air had spoken too soon. With the added weight of Norik, their momentum was spending itself too soon. They began to arc down toward the water below.

"Or not," added Matau.

The Toa Hordika and Rahaga slammed into

the water. Above, their three allies watched with concern. "What do we do now?" asked Whenua.

"Seeing as Norik is the one that knows the way to Keetongu," said Nokama, "we swim!"

She ran and jumped off the ledge, executing a graceful dive into the canal. A moment later, she disappeared beneath the surface of the liquid protodermis.

Whenua looked at Nuju. "Oh, brother."

The two Toa stepped to the edge, steeled themselves, and jumped off.

Sidorak marched boldly through a Coliseum tunnel, Vakama dutifully following behind. The king of the Visorak reflected on what he had accomplished this day. An "engagement" with Roodaka would have many positive effects. As queen of the hordes, she would share equally with Sidorak in the rewards of conquest, making it less likely she would try to undercut his power in future. This ridiculous competition to earn Makuta's favor would end. Best of all, Sidorak would now have standing in Roodaka's land — and given the power of those said to dwell there, that was no small achievement.

Vakama was another matter, of course. Sidorak saw no reason not to trust the Toa Hordika's defection, and it was true that no other horde master would be better suited to anticipate the strategies of Toa. Still, the king was determined that Vakama's ambitions would start and end with being field commander, and not extend to the throne. Sidorak knew from experience how quickly a ruthless being could ascend to power.

"You know, Vakama, you remind me a bit of myself at your age," he said. When Vakama made no reply, he added, "That was a compliment."

"Thank you, my king," Vakama said half-heartedly.

"Think nothing of it. Such is the generosity of my rule," the king continued. "My horde is an obedient one. They will do anything you command. Unless I command differently, of course."

"Of course," Vakama replied.

Sidorak slapped the Toa Hordika on the

back, almost knocking him off his feet. "Good. Now then —"

They stepped out onto the Coliseum observation deck. Assembled below were hundreds of Visorak of every type, waiting for their orders.

"Meet the troops!" boomed Sidorak.

The eyes of the Visorak spiders went from Sidorak to Vakama. Then, as one, they bowed before their new commander. Despite himself, Vakama felt a flush of pride. These were experienced hunters, crack teams that had ravaged a thousand lands, and yet they were prepared to follow his leadership. Where five Toa had scoffed at him, a thousand Visorak were now ready to fight at his command.

"Perhaps you'd like to say a few words?" suggested Sidorak.

Vakama's Hordika side rose in full fury. He gave a roar that shook the Coliseum. The Visorak horde rose to its collective feet and responded with a roar of its own.

From a distance, Roodaka watched the

scene unfold with pleasure. As viceroy, she had limited authority over the horde, and many of the Visorak refused to do anything without Sidorak's stated approval. But now Vakama ruled the horde, and she would rule Vakama.

Sidorak doesn't know it, she thought, *but he just became expendable.*

Toa Hordika flew through an underwater chute at a frightening rate of speed. Unlike the above-ground chutes, this one was still functional, evidently from some power source previously undiscovered by the Matoran.

That explains how the Visorak got to Metru Nui, thought Nokama as she rocketed along. *There must be other chutes under the sea that are still operating, though I can't imagine how.*

Her eyes, more accustomed to seeing underwater than those of the others, detected something strange ahead. The chute curved upward abruptly and seemed to be ruptured in places. She could feel a chill in the water as she drew closer to that spot. The next instant, she was no longer in liquid protodermis, but skidding along a sheet of ice inside the chute!

Water, she could handle — ice was another matter. Unable to check her flight, she went hurtling out of the chute, followed closely by Nuju and Whenua. All three sailed through the air before slamming into a snowbank.

Shaken, Nokama looked around. They were in a white world, so bright it was almost blinding. It looked like Ko-Metru, but a Ko-Metru where the weather had gone mad. "Where are we?" she asked.

"Home," said Nuju.

Whenua shook the snow off himself. "Good. Then you know where we are?"

Nuju looked around. With surprise in his voice, he answered, "No."

Whenua shook his head. "Always watching the stars. But the earth has its secrets, too."

Norik's head suddenly popped out of the canopy of snow above them. "Keetongu has never been found, my friends. It follows that where he lives hasn't been, either."

"I don't believe it." It was Matau's voice, coming from somewhere off to the left. Nokama turned to see the Toa Hordika of Air pulling himself out of a snowdrift and pointing into the distance.

"It *does* sky-touch," he said, in awe.

Norik and the Toa Hordika looked in the direction he was pointing. Liquid protodermis from the ruptured chute had jetted into the air at some point, only to be frozen solid, forming a mountain of crystal-clear ice.

"Come!" shouted Norik, already racing toward its base.

On the floor of the Coliseum, the Visorak horde drilled in preparation for another battle. High above, Vakama watched over his legions, noting every aspect of their movement style and tactics.

"Is it everything I promised you?"

He glanced behind him to see Roodaka approaching, then turned his attention back to the Visorak. "We'll soon find out," he answered.

"Yes, a night of great consequence falls. Be ready — before it is over, many things will change." She gestured toward the approaching Sidorak. "Here comes one of those things now."

The king of the Visorak joined his viceroy and new general. "How is my horde, Vakama?"

"Obedient," answered the Toa Hordika. "And ready, Sidorak, for anything that comes."

"Including Toa?"

"*Especially* Toa," said Vakama.

Sidorak surveyed the scene. As king, he felt he should be issuing some order or offering counsel, but Vakama seemed to have everything well under control. "Well, then ... what now?"

"The hardest part," answered Vakama, gazing out over the city. "We wait."

Using his fang blades, Matau had easily outdistanced the others in climbing the ice mountain. As he neared the summit, he turned back to see Norik, Nokama, Whenua, Onewa, and Nuju struggling to catch up.

"Hurry up, you guys!" he shouted. "It's amazing!"

Matau pulled himself up to the summit. He rose and looked around at the empty, frozen expanse. There was nothing there but ice and more ice.

"Not," he added.

By now, the others had reached the top of the peak as well. The Toa Hordika looked confused — was this what they had made the climb for? Only Norik seemed unconcerned about the apparent lack of any sign of Keetongu.

"Don't be so quick to judge, Matau," the Rahaga said. Then he turned and began speaking to the barren ice and frigid air. "We are sorry to disturb your rest, noble one, but the duty of these Toa requires that they ask for your help."

For a long moment, nothing happened. Matau felt like an idiot. Why had they believed all this talk of lost Rahi with amazing powers? It was all just some Rahaga's imagination at work. More importantly, how were they going to get back?

"May I be judgmental now?" he asked, disgusted.

As if in answer, the mountain began to shake violently, almost knocking the Toa off their feet.

Norik turned to Matau, smiling. "Yes."

What happened next was a sight no one present would ever forget. From the depths of the ice rose a creature unlike any they had seen before. His armor looked as if it had been forged from the sun, and his very presence radiated power. His right arm ended in a whirling array of shields, while his left hand held a wickedly sharp pickax. A hatch in his chest partially concealed a Rhotuka spinner launcher. The Rahi looked over the beings assembled before him with a single great eye.

In a voice that had not been heard by any living being for centuries, the creature said, "Toa."

Norik gazed up at the mighty being who had answered his summons. A part of him wanted this moment to never end, for it was the culmination of so many years of work and hardship.

"Keetongu," he said, the word carrying all the awe, hope, and joy he was feeling.

A long moment of silence followed. Finally, Matau spoke up, saying, "So, big guy, about that favor-gift . . ."

"—All of which is why we came here, and why we need your assistance," Norik finished. "Will you help us get Vakama back?"

The Toa Hordika, Norik, and Keetongu were sitting in the underground cavern that the Rahi called home. It was bitterly cold and damp and the aroma was none too pleasant, but most of the Toa were willing to ignore all that if it meant gaining this powerful new ally.

Keetongu looked at Norik and grunted a simple, "No."

"Well, thanks just the same," said Onewa, already rising and eager to get out of the dark space. "We'll be going, then."

Whenua clamped a hand on his friend's shoulder and kept him still. Keetongu was speaking again, but this time in a language none of the Toa could understand. Only Norik, listening attentively, seemed able to comprehend what was being said.

"Keetongu cannot start a battle on your behalf," Norik translated. "But he can aid those loyal to the three virtues. Those like Toa. In fact, doing so is his sworn duty."

Matau smiled. "So he'll change us back into our good-looking, Toa-hero selves?"

Keetongu looked at the Toa Hordika of Air and said, "No."

"I'm confused," said Whenua.

Keetongu began speaking again. After a few moments, Norik nodded and said, "Of course, of course."

"What is it?" asked Nokama.

"Keetongu sees with one eye what we have not with all of ours," Norik explained. "If you are to save Vakama, you must use your new forms and abilities, not be rid of them."

Matau threw his hands into the air. "So we've come all this way — just to find out we didn't have to come all this way!"

Keetongu made a series of strange sounds. It took the Toa a moment to realize it was laughter.

"He thinks it's funny, too," reported Norik.

"Right. Funny," Matau said bitterly. "That's what I was thinking."

Keetongu spoke to Norik again. The Rahaga said, "Your story and devotion to your friend have touched Keetongu. He says it probably helps that it's the first story he's heard since the time before time. But just the same, he finds your quest worthwhile."

The Rahi grunted. Norik seemed shocked by the sound, so much that he forgot to translate until Matau prodded, "And —?"

"And ...," Norik said quietly, "he would like to offer us his help."

Nokama smiled, feeling for the first time that there might be hope of success after all. She thrust her fist forward. One by one, Nuju, Onewa, Whenua, and Matau met her fist with theirs. She looked at Norik, her eyes holding an unspoken invitation to join them.

"I would be honored," said the Rahaga, adding his fist to the circle.

Matau looked up at Keetongu. "You, too, big guy."

The Rahi extended a hand to complete the circle. Now they were united in a common goal — but no one in the chamber could forget that Vakama was missing. And each, in his or her own way, made a vow to find him and save him from the shadows ... no matter what it took.

*   *   *

Vakama tested his blazer claws for the hundredth time. He was sick of waiting. He wanted to be running, fighting, anything to keep his mind off of where he was and what he was doing.

He had no doubt the other Toa were out there with Norik, plotting against him. They would never understand the choice he had made, or that it was the only way to save the Matoran. *They are fools, like I used to be,* he thought. *Caught up in the image of being a Toa, and the notion that a mask and a tool and some armor make you the equal of anyone you fight.*

A thin, hot flame erupted from his claw. *Well, they don't. Sometimes the odds are too great ... sometimes what's inside the armor isn't strong enough to overcome them. If I fought beside them, we would all die and the Matoran would be lost. This ... this is the only way.*

The Toa Hordika of Fire stared into the mist, trying in vain to spot his former friends.

"Where are they?" asked Roodaka.

She didn't have to wait long for an answer. Something smashed into the Coliseum gates, knocking them off their hinges. A couple of battered Visorak sentries followed, hurled into the arena by whatever had felled the doors. As the smoke cleared, Vakama saw five Toa Hordika march into the Coliseum, looking for all the world as if they had already conquered it.

"Vakama!" shouted Nokama.

Her voice struck a chord in the Toa Hordika of Fire. It had been easy to dismiss his old allies from his heart when they were absent, but now, seeing them again . . . remembering their adventures . . . all he could do was whisper, "Nokama . . ."

Roodaka saw what was happening. She leaned over the rail of the observation platform and said, "Not the one you know, Nokama."

"I didn't hear *him* say that," snapped Matau.

Roodaka looked at Vakama. He did not disappoint her. "She's right," he said. "You're not here for the reason you think."

Whenua pointed up at his former leader. "We came here to save you!"

"The only ones you can save now are

yourselves," Vakama replied. "Bow down and pledge your allegiance to me!"

Off to the side, Sidorak coughed loudly.

"To the Visorak," Vakama added.

Sidorak coughed again.

Vakama finally got the message. "To the Visorak king!"

Onewa took a step forward. "And if we don't?"

The Toa Hordika of Fire raised a blazer claw, the implied threat was obvious to all. "I'll make you."

Nokama looked at her companions. Each of them nodded in turn. They had not come so far only to turn back now, let alone surrender to an apparently demented fire-spitter. She looked back at Vakama, holding her fin barb aloft, and said, "I don't think so."

"Yeah," said Matau, stepping up to stand beside her. "You and what battle-army?"

Vakama reached out and snapped off one of the sharpened flagpoles that lined the observation deck. He hurled it down toward the Toa Hordika, its point burying itself in the ground in front of his former friends.

More than an answer, it was a signal. The Visorak horde emerged from all around the Toa, their numbers rapidly filling the stadium. Once they were all in position, each spider creature activated its Rhotuka spinner, all of them aimed right at the Toa.

"Oh, right," Matau said. "That one."

Nokama willed her own spinner to life. "As we discussed," she said. "Ready . . ."

The other four Toa followed her lead, the energy of their spinners crackling in the misty air. "You really think this is going to work?" asked Matau.

Nokama ignored him. "Aim . . ."

The Toa shifted as one. Their spinners were no longer aimed at the horde, but rather at the uppermost levels of the Coliseum. At Nokama's signal, they each extended a Toa tool into the whirling field of energy. Merged with the spinners, the tools were held fast. Now wherever they went, the Toa Hordika would be pulled along behind.

Nokama glanced at Matau. "Ask me again in a minute."

All around them, the Visorak spinners were making an angry hum like a maddened swarm of fireflyers. Onewa had come to know that sound all too well. It meant they were about to be launched.

"Uh, Nokama?" he said.

The Toa Hordika of Water was watching the Visorak carefully, waiting for the right moment. If she moved too soon, they would change their target and nail the Toa as they ascended. She had to wait until the spiders had committed to their launch, no matter how risky that might be.

Roodaka was growing impatient. The Toa Hordika were at their mercy, surrounded with no way to escape. What was Vakama waiting for? *If you want an enemy ground into the dust, you have to do it yourself,* she decided.

"Fire!" Roodaka shouted.

The Visorak spinners launched, even as their viceroy flipped a switch, causing the observation platform to ascend. Down below, Matau watched with panic as hundreds of spinners flew right toward him.

"What she said!" he shouted.

The five Toa launched their spinners and then held on to their tools for dear life as they were pulled into the air. The Visorak spinners converged on the spot where they had been standing, utterly decimating the ground.

Onewa glanced over his shoulder at the horde and shouted, "Gotcha!" Unfortunately, taking his eyes off where he was going proved to be a bad idea, as he slammed headfirst into the side of the Coliseum.

Nokama, Nuju, and Whenua stuck to the plan. With great effort, they climbed up their tools and mounted the spinners. None of them had ever tried anything like this before—actually riding a wheel of energy—and they all knew it was only the electromagnetic field around the wheels that supported them. The instant the spinners weakened, they would fall to their deaths. For now, though, they were proving quite effective at slicing through Visorak webs.

Nokama's orders had been for all five Toa to head into the Coliseum's maze of hallways, but Matau had other plans. Once he saw they were safely inside, he steered his spinner up toward the observation deck and Vakama.

The time has come to settle things between us, fire-spitter, he said to himself. *I'm coming back down with you . . . or I'm not coming back down.*

Earth-shaking sounds rattled the Coliseum. At first, it had felt like something was advancing toward the structure, but now it was as if that something was pounding on the building itself — a prospect Sidorak did not find comforting.

"Still, that sound," he said uneasily. He reached out and flipped the switch, bringing the observation platform to a halt. Leaning over the side, he saw something that froze his black heart.

It was Keetongu, body radiating raw power,

climbing up the wall of the Coliseum. With the horde in hot pursuit of the Toa Hordika, there had been no Visorak to warn of his approach.

"What is that?" asked Sidorak, shocked.

Vakama glanced over the side, seemingly unconcerned. "I guess it's Keetongu."

"But Keetongu doesn't exist!"

Vakama met the Visorak king's gaze and said flatly, "I guess you're wrong about that." The Toa Hordika of Fire turned his attention to Roodaka, saying, "I'll take care of him."

She reached out a hand to stop him. "No, Vakama. It is not your place." Roodaka smiled and extended her clawed hand to Sidorak. "It is that of a king."

A million thoughts flew through Sidorak's mind at once. Facing Keetongu would, of course, be potentially suicidal. But refusing to do so would mean losing the respect of Roodaka, perhaps even being so shamed that the horde would no longer obey him. In the end, he really had no choice, and he knew it.

And so did Roodaka.

Sidorak drew himself up proudly and took his viceroy's hand. "If Keetongu wasn't a myth before, he soon will be."

Roodaka and Sidorak headed for the platform's exit and a confrontation with the legendary Rahi beast, leaving Vakama behind.

"Where is my place?" he asked.

Roodaka never looked back as she said, "The future, Vakama. The near future. As I told you before . . . be ready."

Then they were gone. Vakama walked back to the railing, muttering, "The future — I wish it would hurry up and get here."

"It has!"

Vakama turned barely in time to see Matau, being pulled along by his spinner, flying toward him. Before the Toa Hordika of Fire could react, Matau had grabbed him and yanked him off the platform and into the air. They soared high above the Coliseum, Vakama struggling all the while.

"Put me down!" he yelled.

But Matau had no intention of letting go. It was only when Vakama finally managed to wrench

Matau's fang blade loose from the spinner's field that their ascent stopped abruptly. Without the Rhotuka's power to keep them aloft, the two Toa Hordika plunged toward the Coliseum's central spire. Together they smashed through the dome of the atrium that crowned the spire, landing amid its fragile framework.

It was Matau who made it to his feet first. "You wanted down," he snarled, "you got down."

Vakama leapt from the debris, eyes blazing, pain and anger bringing the Hordika side of him to the surface.

"Your place is here, Vakama. Now. With us," said Matau. "We're here to rescue the Matoran."

Vakama's answer was a growl of rage.

"You remember, don't you?" Matau asked hopefully.

This time, his old friend's response was an impossibly fast leap that sent him crashing into Matau.

Keetongu had almost reached the top of the central spire of the Coliseum. No Visorak had dared challenge him. Warriors they might be, but fools they were not.

Not everyone ran from the Rahi, however. A bolt of pure shadow struck him in mid-climb, tearing him free of the building and sending him toward the ground. Halfway down, he slammed his sharpened tool into the wall, checking his plunge.

High above, Roodaka stood, wisps of dark energy still swirling around her fingertips. Seeing that her prey had somehow managed to save himself, she muttered, "I'm almost impressed."

Worried, she was not — she and Sidorak were in a perfect position to pick off the Rahi beast at their leisure. Taking careful aim, Roodaka let loose another blast. This one shattered his tool. Again, Keetongu fell.

It is only right, she thought. *A legendary Rahi must meet a legendary death, after all.*

9

What thoughts went through the mind of the Rahi called Keetongu as he plunged toward the Coliseum floor far below? Did he wonder if this was some sad trick of fate, that he should emerge after having been hidden for so long, only to die? Did he fear for the safety of the Toa Hordika once he was gone? Did he face his end with courage, or the blind, unthinking panic of a beast?

There was no way for anyone to find out before he struck the tiled floor like a meteor, creating a massive crater. The impact triggered the last reserves of power in the arena, activating the floor and causing individual tiles to rise and fall like ocean waves. When it finally ground to a halt, the Coliseum pavement was a tiered field of random heights and treacherous drops.

"Well, that's that," said Sidorak.

"No!" snapped Roodaka. Then, realizing Sidorak was looking at her in surprise, added gently, "I mean . . . shouldn't we be certain?"

Sidorak glanced down at the crater and the unmoving Keetongu. Emboldened by the victory, he said, "If doing so would make you feel better, my soon queen."

He headed inside the spire to make the journey down to the arena floor. Roodaka followed, her soft comment dripping with insincerity and acid. "Yes, if only you'll protect me."

Matau staggered toward the narrow ledge that surrounded the atrium. Another step, and he would be nothing but a green smear on the ground so far below. Not that Vakama seemed to care about that, given how he was advancing on his fellow Toa.

"I said I wanted to talk, Vakama, not anger-fight!"

"I don't take orders from you," growled Vakama. "I give them!"

For the first time, Matau truly saw how his

old friend had changed. Whatever Vakama's reasons for allying with the Visorak — good ones, or bad — it seemed that he had now plunged so deeply into shadow that he had lost himself.

"What's happened to you?"

Vakama snarled, a savage grin on his face.

"You know, outside of the obvious," Matau added.

"Don't fight it, Matau," Vakama replied, in a voice brimming with darkness. "It is our destiny."

Before Matau could answer, Vakama charged again. Knocked off balance, Matau fell over the ledge. But his Hordika reflexes saved him as he caught hold of a bust of Sidorak. Dangling helplessly from it, he could only watch as his attacker advanced, ready to bring their conflict — and Matau's life — to an end.

Sidorak and Roodaka stood over the fallen Keetongu. The beast lay unmoving, his armor blackened and scorched by the viceroy's power. He looked like he would no longer be a menace to an Archives mole, let alone to the ruler of the Visorak.

"On your feet, thing," snarled Sidorak.

In response, Keetongu tried to rise. But the blasts and the impact were too much. He slumped down again.

"Whatever," muttered the Visorak king. "The final blow is yours, Roodaka."

"Just like all the others?"

Her tone was no longer respectful and submissive — in fact, it sounded positively insolent. Sidorak turned to find another surprise: Roodaka was walking away.

"Where are you going?" he demanded. "Finish him!"

"You're the great king, Sidorak," she challenged. "You do it."

Sidorak looked away from her, back to Keetongu. The Rahi had finally made it to his feet, battered, bruised . . . and very, very angry.

"But I can't defeat him myself," Sidorak pleaded in a harsh whisper.

Roodaka smiled. "I know."

It was then, even as she disappeared among the pillars of protodermis, that Sidorak finally knew. She had engineered it all. Her blasts had been calculated to wound the Keetongu, but not to kill, leaving Sidorak at the mercy of a maddened Rahi. And why? Because there was another way for Roodaka to take control of the horde, one much faster and easier than a marriage of convenience.

The death of the king.

A shadow fell on Sidorak, but now he realized it was not the shadow of Keetongu. It was the shadow of his own doom. The fate he had visited upon so many others over the centuries was now to be visited upon him. As Keetongu raised his great fist, Sidorak wondered if his viceroy realized that in a way she was acting in the interests of justice — a concept she despised.

"Roodaka," the king said weakly as the blow fell. As last words go, not very memorable. But in the moment of his death, Sidorak did something he had never done before: He gave credit where credit was due.

Roodaka heard the sound of rending metal, a sign that the battle had ended the way she knew it would. So engrossed was she by the thought, she never noticed hundreds of Visorak eyes narrowing at the sight of her betrayal. "The king is dead," she said, smiling.

Her gaze drifted to the top of the spire, where Vakama was about to seal his fate by killing a fellow Toa. Once that act was completed, there would be no going back for the Toa Hordika of Fire. He would belong to the shadows.

"Long live the king," said Roodaka, a peal of dark laughter on her lips.

Matau was being extremely stubborn. He wouldn't surrender. He wouldn't fall and die. Vakama was determined that his old ally would do one or the other, and he was no longer certain he cared which. Figuring what the Toa Hordika of Air needed was a little motivation, Vakama stepped on his fingers.

"You're weak, brother," he hissed.

Matau winced at the pain, but somehow hung on. "You're right, Vakama — I am weak. Nokama, Whenua, Onewa, Nuju — we all are."

"So, at last you see the truth."

"Yeah, I guess I do," Matau answered. "I've made a lot of fool-mistakes lately, Vakama. That's what happens when you're brave-tough enough to make decisions. I understand that now."

"Forgive me if I don't believe that, coming from you," Vakama said, making no effort to hide his bitterness. He raised an armored fist, snarling, "Now let's finish this."

"Wait!" yelled Matau.

Vakama came to a sudden stop, the final blow still poised to strike his former friend. "Not for long."

"I just want you to know that — I'm sorry. For ever-doubting you . . . you see, Vakama, that's the reason we're so deep-weak. We don't have you."

Was that a flicker of awareness in Vakama's eyes? Some remnant of his Toa spirit fighting to break through the shroud of Hordika rage? Matau wasn't sure, but he saw his opening and was going to take it. If Vakama killed him, well, at least he would have had his say.

"Our Toa-strength comes from our unity, Vakama," he said urgently. "Which means you can't be ever-strong without us, either — no matter what some screw-brained monster like Roodaka tells you."

Vakama's fist began to shake. Matau's words were forcing him to remember feelings he had buried. He struggled to remember the reasons he had allied himself with Roodaka — they had been good reasons, he was sure — but instead he found only questions. Why had he been so filled with rage, beyond what even the Hordika mutation should have caused? Why had his power to see visions of the future failed him?

"I'm better — stronger — alone," he said. Even in his ears, the words sounded hollow.

"I don't trust-believe that. And I don't think

you do, either." Matau looked up at Vakama again. "Things change — but you'll always be my friend and Toa-brother. And something more — something it took all of this for me to learn-see." Matau's eyes locked on those of Vakama. "You're our leader, Vakama. You're *my* leader."

The Toa Hordika of Fire began to lower his fist. He wished Matau would shut up and stop confusing him. It would be so easy to silence his chatter. One blow, and no more Matau. Why couldn't he do it? Why did he even want to do it? What was wrong with his mind?

"And in case you've quick-forgotten, we've got a job to do," Matau continued. "A Toa-duty. One we have to work together to get through."

"The Matoran," answered Vakama. Did Matau think he had forgotten them? Everything he had done, he had done for . . .

No. Wait. That isn't right, Vakama thought. *How would killing Matau possibly help the Matoran? I was going to order the Matoran freed . . . the Toa freed . . . and here I am, about to swat one like I would a fireflyer.*

"I knew you'd remember," Matau said, smiling. "If you ask me, rescuing the Matoran is maybe the reason we were made Toa-heroes. Our destiny. One that's better than any other someone else could offer you."

Mata Nui, why won't he just shut up? thought Vakama. *All that chatter, all those words ... they never stop.*

"I didn't ask," the Toa Hordika of Fire said, his expression darkening.

Matau knew he had maybe pushed too hard, too fast. *Holding on above a high-fall will make you impatient,* he thought.

"You're true-right, you didn't," he said to Vakama. "I guess I just needed you to hear it. And if there's any of the Toa-hero Vakama I know left in there, he'll know what to do with it . . . and what's going to happen next."

"Matau! Don't!"

But Vakama's cry was too late. The Toa Hordika of Air had let go of the bust of Sidorak and was falling to his death, as surely as if Vakama had pushed him.

In that instant, Vakama knew he had to make a decision. He could hear Roodaka, promising him power beyond imagining in return for betraying his fellow Toa. He could hear Turaga Lhikan saying, "I am proud to have called you brother, Toa Vakama"—those were the last words that hero had spoken before dying for Metru Nui.

Matau was right, Vakama realized. *I do know what to do.*

10

Nokama, Nuju, Onewa, and Whenua made their way through the twisting corridors of the Coliseum. Their goal was the subterranean vault in which the sleeping Matoran were kept, locked inside silver spheres.

"Keep moving," urged Nokama. "We're almost there."

"The Matoran are in the next chamber," said Nuju.

The four Toa Hordika rushed into the vault and past a pair of massive pillars to reach the storage racks. All around them were stacks of Matoran spheres. The knowledge that they were so close to completing their mission, despite all the obstacles they had faced, filled the Toa with a feeling of triumph.

"We made it!" shouted Onewa.

But Whenua was not ready to join the celebration. His enhanced Hordika senses told him something was wrong. It was what felt like a draft in a room far removed from any outside exits. With a shudder, he realized that it was not a draft — it was something breathing.

The pillars moved, revealing themselves to be huge legs. The ceiling shifted as a massive creature bent down, the monstrous face of a Kahgarak coming into view. The Toa had seen these elite Visorak guardians before, but never one quite so large.

"And that's a good thing?" said Whenua.

Onewa shook his head. "We are so gonna feel this . . ."

With a sharp hiss, the Kahgarak attacked. An instant later, the Toa Metru were flying through the Coliseum wall and out into the center of the arena. Debris rained down around them, half-burying them in a pit.

"Weren't we just here?" asked Nuju, dazed.

Nokama glanced up. Visorak of every type

were fast converging on the pit. The Toa were completely surrounded.

"On your feet," she barked to the others. "Now!"

Standing back to back, the Toa Hordika prepared for what would surely be their last stand.

Matau heard the wind whistle past him as he fell toward the arena floor. Letting go had been a desperate gamble, and it appeared headed for failure.

"What a dark-mess," he muttered. "I was stupid to think I could quick-save Vakama."

"You did, Matau."

The Toa Hordika of Air looked up. There was Vakama, plunging down after him, arms outstretched. "Vakama!"

"Yes," said the Toa Hordika of Fire. "The one you know."

Now they were both falling, but Matau hardly noticed. With his brother Toa at his side, he suddenly felt like they could overcome anything.

"Well, feel free to return the favor, brother," he said. "There's no shortage of Toa-heroes who need saving."

Vakama smiled. "Yes. I have a plan for that." He grabbed Matau.

"Great," replied Matau. "But do you have a thought-plan to make us —"

His sentence was cut off by the abrupt halt in their fall. Puzzled, Matau looked up and saw that Vakama had a strand of Visorak webbing tied around his ankle. Its elasticity had stopped their plunge without snapping them in two, for which Matau was grateful. He was less so about what was going to happen next.

Stretched to its limit, the webbing suddenly snapped back, sending the two Toa hurtling up toward the observation deck.

The five Rahaga struggled in vain to undo their bonds. They had seen the valiant fight the Toa Hordika were putting up against the hordes, futile as it might be. They knew once the Toa were downed, Roodaka would have no further use for her "bait."

"It's no use," said Bomonga. "What would Norik do?"

None of the Rahaga had an answer for that. Then a reply came from an unexpected direction — up above!

"Watch, and I'll show you!"

The Rahaga followed the direction of the voice to see their missing friend flying toward them on top of his energy spinner.

"Norik!" shouted Kualus, overjoyed.

"I knew you'd come for us!" said Iruini. "What took you so long?"

Norik landed and unlimbered his staff, using its edge to slice through the Rahaga's bonds. "My flying isn't what it used to be. I'm not exactly a Toa, you know."

"Not exactly," agreed Bomonga.

"Now then," said Norik, "let's go help those who are."

* * *

The Rahaga reached the arena floor just as the Visorak's determined attack was about to overwhelm the four Toa Hordika.

"This is it," said Nokama, almost too tired to lift her fin barbs. "May the Great Spirit welcome us."

"Mind if we lend a hand?" shouted Norik.

"Or twelve of them?" said Iruini.

"We're going to need them all," answered Onewa.

In truth, they were going to need far more than the help of the Rahaga to win the day. The Visorak came in waves, and even with the addition of new allies, it was only a matter of time before the Toa's defenses were broken.

"Norik, even with your help —" Nokama began.

"I know, noble Nokama," the Rahaga answered. "And it's all right."

Roodaka's voice cut through the din of battle. "I'm glad to hear you have made your peace, Rahaga."

The viceroy of the Visorak was riding atop

the Kahgarak, the horde assembled around her. If the Visorak were less than enthusiastic to be following the murderer of their king, they were keeping it to themselves.

Roodaka dismounted and looked at the four Toa. "But first, you have something I want."

"What more could you possibly take from us?" asked Nokama.

The viceroy smiled. "Your elemental powers. Earth. Stone. Ice. Water. Fire already belongs to me." Then her smile abruptly vanished. "Wait — one's missing."

Matau landed hard in front of her. "Yeah. That would be me."

Vakama followed right after him, taking up a position next to Roodaka. "Thank you, Vakama," said the viceroy. "Now about those powers . . ."

Matau willed his Rhotuka spinner to life. Nuju, Nokama, Onewa, and Whenua followed his lead. "You want 'em so bad?" snarled the Toa Hordika of Air. "Take 'em!"

The five Rhotuka spinners slammed into Roodaka, unleashing their elemental fury. She was staggered by the onslaught, but not felled. Instead, her response was chilling laughter.

"All right," said Matau. "Who quick-launched the tickle spinner?"

"Fools!" snapped Roodaka. "Your powers are nothing." She gestured to Vakama, who still stood silently beside her. "If they are not united."

Roodaka raised a claw and summoned the dark energy that coursed through her. "And as Vakama stands with me —"

"Actually . . . ," said the Toa Hordika of Fire.

Roodaka turned to see him activating a fire spinner, aimed squarely at her.

"I wanted to talk to you about that," he finished.

For only a moment, the viceroy showed fear. Then she regained her composure and gestured toward the horde. "You can defeat me, Vakama, but not all of them. Strike me down, and they will surely destroy you and your friends. Think about it."

"I have," answered Vakama. "And seeing as you convinced Sidorak to have the horde obey me ..." He turned to the assembled legions of spider creatures. "Get out of here, all of you. You're free. That's an order."

For a split second, the outcome was in doubt. The Visorak had been conditioned for years to blindly follow the orders of their leader. Sidorak had led them to conquest after conquest, and Roodaka was his successor by virtue of his death. Ordinarily, even the orders of their commander could not make them turn on their leader. But too many of them had seen Roodaka lure Sidorak to his death ... and betrayal could not, must not, be rewarded with loyalty. Without so much as a glance in her direction, the horde dispersed, abandoning her as she had abandoned their king.

"Traitors!" Roodaka screamed after them.

"You can't betray someone you're enslaved to," said Vakama.

"And to think I thought you could be king," she sneered.

"I lead only those who choose to follow me," Vakama replied. "That's the difference between being a leader and being a tyrant. A certain Toa taught me that. And something else . . . our destinies are not written in stone, set in place. They are something we have to find for ourselves."

His spinner rose and hovered in the air. "I've found mine."

Everything happened at lightning speed. In the instant before the spinner was sent on its way, Roodaka pried open a plate on her armor to reveal an ebony stone. Seeing this, Norik rushed forward and screamed, "No, Vakama! Don't!"

It was too late. Vakama's spinner crossed the short distance between him and Roodaka and struck her. Its energies combined with those she had already absorbed, setting off a chain reaction. There was an explosion of brilliant light so bright it blinded them all. When the glare had faded, Roodaka was no more, with only shards of the stone remaining to mark her passing.

"Vakama, you have no idea what you've just done," said Norik.

"Her heartstone," Vakama replied.

"Yes, carved from the same protodermis

you sealed the Makuta in. In destroying it, you've broken the seal."

"And set Makuta free," concluded the Toa Hordika of Fire. He looked at his brothers and sister, safe and together once more. "For some reason, he doesn't scare me anymore."

Vakama turned at the sound of an impact behind him. He saw Keetongu on the ground, spent from his efforts against Sidorak and Roodaka. The Toa Hordika gathered by the Rahi's side.

"You owe me nothing, Keetongu, especially in light of all you've already done," said Vakama. "But my duty requires that I ask — will you change us back?"

Keetongu's answer came in his own language. Norik translated, "He wants to know why you would want that, now that you have made peace with the beast within? That you might even be the better for it..."

"There's a promise we must be our old selves in order to keep," Vakama answered.

"Then so will you be," said Keetongu.

Vakama held out his fist. The other five

Toa Hordika touched theirs to his, forming once more the circle of six.

"All right, big guy," Matau said to Keetongu. "Hit it."

Keetongu drew upon his unique power and released his energy in a wave, letting it wash over the mutated forms of the Toa Hordika. The Rahaga looked on, silently imploring the Great Spirit to make things right once more.

The door to the Matoran vault opened once more. This time, it was Toa Metru who stepped over the threshold, not Toa Hordika.

"Time to wake up, my friends," Vakama said, looking around at the multitude of spheres. "We're going home."

It took many hours of labor by the Toa, the Rahaga, and Keetongu to remove the spheres from the vault. They were then loaded into the airships the Toa had constructed for just this occasion when they were Hordika.

"Nice ships," Matau commented, looking over his own handiwork.

"Just don't crash them this time," replied Onewa, smiling.

Nearby, Vakama and Norik stood together. The Toa Metru of Fire took a long, last look at his city, knowing it might well be years before he saw it again. "I guess this is it," he said.

"No, Vakama," said Norik. "This is just a different beginning."

"Of what?"

Norik smiled. "I wouldn't dream of spoiling it for you."

"Well, whatever it is, thank you."

"You are most welcome, Vakama," replied the Rahaga. "But it is I who should be thanking you."

"I don't understand."

Norik smiled broadly. "It's not every day I get to see a legend, you know."

The Toa of Fire nodded toward Keetongu. "Yes, he is quite a sight."

"Indeed," the Rahaga replied. "But I wasn't talking about Keetongu."

It took a moment before Norik's words

sank in. The Rahaga was right — what they had accomplished would live in legend, from this day forward. "The Great Rescue," said Vakama.

"It's funny," said the Rahaga. "You spend your whole life chasing something, only to find when you finally catch it that the pursuit was what was important. That it's changed you. That you'll never be exactly the same."

Vakama nodded. "I guess I've changed, too."

Norik placed a hand on the Toa's armored shoulder. "And in doing so, freed us Rahaga to be what we are ... knowing that the new world and its Matoran are in most capable hands. Which means the last time I will ever use this gesture ...," Norik finished, holding out his fist in the Toa salute, "is to say thanks. I like that."

"Me, too," said Vakama, meeting the Rahaga's fist with his own.

The small fleet of ships had lifted off and were heading out to sea. Aftershocks from Makuta's earthquake had widened the gap in the Great

Barrier, and Vakama believed new tunnels might be found leading to the surface. For a change, no one argued with him.

Riding in the lead ship, Nokama, Vakama, and the other Toa looked down over the city.

"Will you miss it?" asked the Toa of Water.

Vakama glanced down and saw the Rahaga and Keetongu on the observation deck of the Coliseum, their eyes tracking the slow passage of the ships. "Some things," he answered.

As they neared the Great Barrier, Onewa pointed down to the rocks, alarmed. "Makuta! He's gone!"

Vakama could see that he was right. The protodermis prison was shattered and the master of shadows had disappeared. "Not for long," he said. "I imagine we'll be seeing him again very soon."

"And when we do?"

"We'll find a way to defeat him," said Vakama, steering the ship toward the rift in the barrier. "Because that's what Toa do."

EPILOGUE

"...Because that's what Toa do."

With those final words, Turaga Vakama brought his tale to an end. With one smooth motion, he scooped up the stones from the Amaja Circle. Tahu Nuva took particular note of how he handled the black stone that represented Makuta, the sole surviving shard from that entity's prison of long ago.

"I was right," the Turaga said. "Makuta would follow us here, and threaten to cast our new world and all who came to call it home into everlasting shadow."

Jaller, still caught up in the tale, could barely contain himself. "And ...?"

Vakama smiled. "I believe you already know

that story, Jaller. Come now, enough of old legends for one day."

The Turaga rose and walked away, followed by the Toa Nuva, Takanuva, Jaller, and Hahli. "Where are we going?" asked the Ga-Matoran Chronicler.

"To make new ones," answered the hero of Metru Nui.

APPENDIX: ORIGIN OF THE RAHAGA

From the Chronicles of Takua, as related by Turaga Vakama:

As we prepare to start our journey back to the city of Metru Nui, I cannot help but remember the Rahaga. I wonder if they are still in my homeland, or if they have moved on to continue their work elsewhere. Of all the beings I have encountered, they were among the wisest and bravest. And were it not for them, neither I, my fellow Turaga, nor the Matoran who walk Mata Nui today would be here.

Rahaga Norik rarely wanted to talk about his past. Fortunately, Rahaga Iruini was not so close-mouthed. It was from him that Matau learned the

Rahaga had once been Toa in another land — and not just any Toa. Clad in armor forged from precious metals, and wielding both Toa tools and Rhotuka launchers, they were the elite. Each of the six wore a Kanohi mask forged in the shapes worn by the great heroes of the past. Their duty: Protect Makuta, he who was sworn to protect and defend all Matoran.

They did their job nobly and well. Ironically, they were most often called on to defend Makuta against Rahi attacks (for so powerful a being could not dirty his hands fighting beasts). Believing him to be a good and honorable servant of the will of Mata Nui, Norik and his Toa did not hesitate to aid him.

Then came the day the light of truth dawned, and the Toa were confronted by a horrible reality. Makuta, and the Brotherhood to which he belonged, were not protecting Matoran. They were oppressing and enslaving them. Even the very masks Norik and the others wore had been forged by Matoran working under threat of punishment — or worse. In addition, the

Brotherhood of Makuta had allied itself with a foul mercenary band known as Dark Hunters. They converted the Exo-Toa mechanoids, first built as guardians of the Matoran, into sentries for their own fortresses.

Burning for justice and revenge, the Toa mounted an attack on a Brotherhood base. Arrayed against them were Dark Hunters and Exo-Toa, prepared to sacrifice all in the service of their dark masters. Separated in the conflict, the Toa fell one by one, but not at the hands of these enemies. No, they were felled by treacherous attacks from the shadows by Roodaka.

Finally, only Norik and Iruini remained. Cunning in their strategy and absolutely fearless in their actions, they succeeded in driving off the Dark Hunters and destroying most of the Exo-Toa. Makuta battled them to a stalemate until he, too, left the field, badly weakened. Now the two Toa had to find their companions.

Find them, they did — shrunken, weakened, turned into monstrous mockeries of Turaga. In what she no doubt regarded as a fine jest, Roodaka had mutated them, giving them the heads of Rahkshi and twisted bodies that would frighten all who saw them. Creatures such as these, she believed, would be shunned by any Matoran they approached. Their days as heroes would be over.

Relying on stealth, Norik and Iruini were able to rescue their friends. But they were discovered by Sidorak and Roodaka and struck by her mutation spinners. Strangely, she then allowed them to escape, perhaps convinced they would never prove a danger to her. Six who had once been powerful Toa were now Rahaga.

At first, they were grief stricken over the change. But Kualus and Norik rallied them. "Our bodies have been changed," said Kualus, "but not our hearts. Not our spirits. No matter how we look, every breath we take, we take as heroes in the service of Mata Nui."

Norik gave them new purpose: to find Keetongu, a mythical Rahi said to have the power to counteract any attack. Only he might have a hope of defeating Sidorak and Roodaka. Some, like Iruini, doubted that this being even existed. Still, they agreed to follow Norik's lead, knowing that unity was essential to the Rahaga's survival.

From that day to this, the Rahaga have wandered from island to island, seeking Keetongu and studying the ways of the Rahi. Often, their efforts have brought them into conflict with the Visorak hordes, and many a beast has been saved from certain death by the Rahaga. Sidorak has vowed to destroy them, while Roodaka wonders whether there is some way to use them to further her own ends.

At last, their journey brought the Rahaga to Metru Nui. Knowing the Visorak must inevitably find their way to the city of legends, they hid in the Archives, observing with horror as their ancient enemy, Makuta, returned and rained destruction on the city. They saw the valiant efforts of the Toa Metru that led to his defeat. And they noted with dread that the heroes then left the city, leaving it defenseless before the Visorak horde.

By the time the Toa returned, the Visorak were in control of Metru Nui. Worse, the Toa fell into a trap and were mutated into Toa Hordika. The Rahaga could wait no longer. Risking discovery by Sidorak, they rescued my friends and me. They armed us with truth and gave us the will to fight on.

Whether they wait for us still in Metru Nui or not, Takua, they deserve to be remembered as the greatest of Toa.

For more information on the Rahaga, Roodaka, Sidorak, the Brotherhood of Makuta, and the entire BIONICLE universe, don't miss the BIONICLE Encyclopedia, coming this fall from Scholastic.

Read on for a sneak peak.

BOHROK (BOH-rock): Insectlike mech-anoids who menaced the island of MATA NUI (2) shortly after the TOA arrived there. Each Bohrok contained a KRANA which provided additional power as well as direction to the machine. The krana, in turn, were in mental contact with the BAHRAG who were the ultimate authority over the Bohrok swarms. Bohrok nests extended from below the surface of Mata Nui to below the city of METRU NUI. Each nest was home to hundreds of Bohrok and BOHROK-VA. There were six known breeds of Bohrok: TAHNOK, GAHLOK, NUHVOK, LEHVAK, KOHRAK, and PAHRAK.

History

The first recorded encounter between MATORAN and Bohrok occurred in Metru Nui, when ONU-MATORAN miners stumbled upon a nest filled with sleeping Bohrok. Not certain what the creatures were or why they could not be awakened, the miners turned the Bohrok over to the ARCHIVES. They were put on display and at the same time studied by Matoran researchers. (The name "Bohrok" came from a word carved in the wall of the nest.)

Their first discovery was that the Bohrok themselves were completely inorganic and not "alive" in the sense that Matoran understand life. They also learned that the dormant krana inside them were completely organic and living creatures, although the connection between krana and Bohrok was not yet known. Interestingly, an examination of the Bohrok revealed no traces of any assembly. An Onu-Matoran archivist, MAVRAH, theorized that perhaps the Bohrok were not built, but were in fact originally biomechanical creatures that had somehow evolved to the point where all organic matter was lost. It would have meant going from possibly a living, thinking being to a form of artificial life incapable of independent thought.

Look For The All-New Movie

BIONICLE 3
WEB OF SHADOWS

Only On DVD
Fall 2005

Go to
www.bionicle.com
for updates